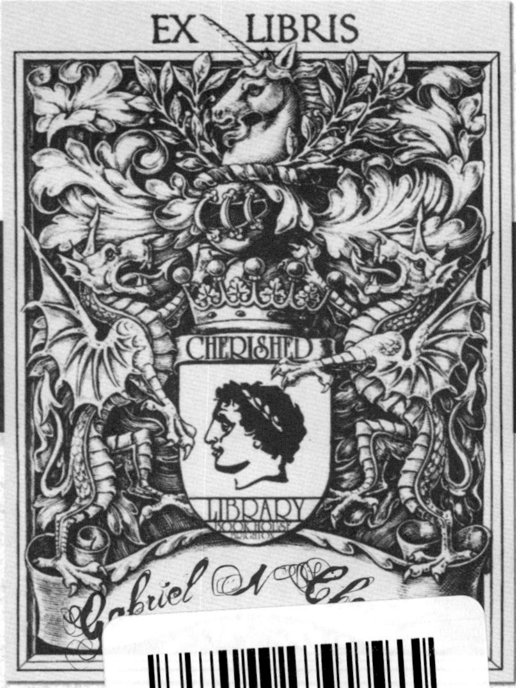
EX LIBRIS
CHERISHED
LIBRARY

England

A Very Peculiar History™

Volume 2

'This blessed plot, this earth,
this realm, this England.'

William Shakespeare, *Richard II*

To my daughter, Alex
IG

Editor: Stephen Haynes
Editorial assistants: Rob Walker, Mark Williams

Published in Great Britain in MMXIII by
Book House, an imprint of
The Salariya Book Company Ltd
25 Marlborough Place, Brighton BN1 1UB
www.salariya.com
www.book-house.co.uk

HB ISBN-13: 978-1-908973-37-5 vol. 1
978-1-908973-38-2 vol. 2
978-1-908973-39-9 vol. 3
978-1-908973-41-2 boxed set

1 3 5 7 9 8 6 4 2

A CIP catalogue record for this book is available
from the British Library.
Printed and bound in Dubai.
Printed on paper from sustainable sources.

Visit
www.salariya.com
for our online catalogue and
free interactive web books.

England
A Very Peculiar History™

Volume 2
From the Wars of the Roses to the
Industrial Revolution

By
Ian Graham

Created and designed by
David Salariya

'When a man is tired of London, he is tired of life; for there is in London all that life can afford.'
Samuel Johnson (1709–1784)

'This England never did, nor never shall, lie at the proud foot of a conqueror.'
William Shakespeare, *King John*

'The English never yield, and though driven back and thrown into confusion, they always return to the fight, thirsting for vengeance as long as they have breath for life.'
Giovanni Mocenigo,
Venetian ambassador to France, 1588

'In England there are 60 different religions, and only one sauce!'
Domenico Caracciola (1752–1799),
Neapolitan diplomat

Contents

Ten things to thank the early modern English for

1. **America** The British prompted the creation of the modern United States by irritating the colonists so much that they proclaimed their independence and built their own country.

2. **Flushing toilets** Surely England's greatest gift to the world, the flushing toilet was invented by Sir John Harington in 1596 and presented by him to his godmother, Queen Elizabeth I. It was only moderately successful.

3. **The English language** Conquering countries all over the world and exporting the English language, education, legal system and government to them (whether they wanted them or not) ensured that English became one of the most widely spoken languages in the world.

4. **Modern theatre** The blossoming of theatre in the first Elizabethan age left a legacy of great works that are still appreciated today.

5. **Accurate navigation** John Harrison's marine chronometers (unprecedentedly accurate clocks) enabled explorers and adventurers to figure out where they were in the world and find their way home safely.

6. **The Royal Navy** During the reign of Henry VIII, the English made themselves so unpopular with France and Spain that there was a constant threat of invasion. Their response was to build the world's most powerful navy, the Royal Navy, to protect themselves.

7. **Spelling and grammar** The rules for English usage were rather fluid until Dr Samuel Johnson's *Dictionary of the English Language* was published in 1755. Many of his spelling preferences are still standard orthography today.

8. **The United Kingdom** Hmm... If you're Scottish, Welsh or Irish, you may have mixed feelings about this one.

9. **The Agricultural Revolution** Selective breeding, improved crop rotation (an idea borrowed from the Dutch) and the use of newly invented machines made it easier to feed the growing cities. This in turn helped to make the Industrial Revolution possible.

10. **The Industrial Revolution** The English changed the way the world produced goods and transported them. For better or worse, we are still living with the consequences.

Putting early modern England on the map

1. Battle of Towton, 1461: the biggest and bloodiest ever fought on English soil
2. Battle of Bosworth Field, 1485: Richard III is killed and Henry Tudor becomes king
3. The Solent, 1545: the *Mary Rose* sinks during an attack on a French fleet
4. Stratford upon Avon, 1564: William Shakespeare is born
5. Fotheringay Castle, 1587: Mary, Queen of Scots is executed on the order of Queen Elizabeth I after being convicted of treason
6. Tilbury, 1588: Queen Elizabeth I gives a rousing speech to prepare her army for an expected Spanish invasion
7. Great Fire of London, 1666, destroys thousands of houses
8. Brixham, 1688: William III lands in England and takes the throne from James II, the last Stuart king
9. Glencoe, 1692: members of the MacDonald clan are massacred on the orders of the Secretary of State
10. Battle of Culloden, 1746: Hanoverian government forces end the Jacobite challenge
11. Isle of Skye, 1746: Bonnie Prince Charlie takes refuge here, helped by Flora MacDonald
12. Bridgewater Canal, 1761: the first major transport canal in England
13. Coalbrookdale, 1779: the world's first arch bridge made from cast iron, giving the nearby town its name, Ironbridge

England on the cusp of the modern era was not always a comfortable place to be

TURBULENT TIMES

Our story begins in the early 1400s. England, a country forged from warring kingdoms that joined forces to repel Viking invaders, has emerged as one of the most powerful nations of Western Europe. Under its great warrior king, Henry V, England has been victorious against the French at the Battle of Agincourt in 1415. Over the next 350 years, English troops and sailors will fight many more battles at home and abroad; kings and queens will fight for the throne and then fight to keep it; and ordinary people will do their best to survive.

Grabbing power

In the early 1400s, the king was an absolute ruler, although it paid him to listen to the advice of courtiers and noblemen. A king who ignored the barons and earls could be in for a tricky time, because he relied on them to provide the men, weaponry and money he needed when he wanted to fight a war.

When the king needed the nobility to come up with the goods, he called a Great Council of noblemen and clergy (monarchs have always liked to feel that they have God on their side). The English Parliament grew out of these Great Councils. As monarchs came and went, Parliament took every opportunity to grab more power for itself at the expense of the monarch. By the time this part of the story of England ends, around 1800, power will have shifted almost completely from the monarch to Parliament. Parliament will hold the real power in the land, and the monarch will be able to act only on the advice of the prime minister.

Who's next?

One question that comes up time and time again in English history is: who is going to be the next king or queen? In theory, it's simple: the eldest son of the monarch inherits the throne. (Even today, daughters can inherit only when there is no son available, but this rule is almost certainly about to change.) However, some kings caused problems by not having a son, so the next monarch had to be chosen from others with a claim to the throne. And, as it became less important for a monarch to lead his troops into battle, even women were allowed to take the throne sometimes.

When two or more people staked rival claims to the crown, the loser often met his or her end at the hands of an executioner. Claim the throne and lose, and you would likely pay for it with your head. Disputed succession could lead to warfare, sometimes on an international scale, so that when the English weren't fighting over their own royal succession, they were often fighting in Europe over succession rights in another country.

Doing Battle

In the early 15th century, where the story told in this volume begins, kings and noblemen (including noblemen who wanted to be king) often got their way by force of arms. They raised armies of knights and thousands of ordinary people, and set them against each other with pikes, swords, axes and arrows. In the bloodiest battle ever fought on English soil – the Battle of Towton (North Yorkshire) in 1461 – 30,000 men were killed.

But by the Battle of Bosworth (Leicestershire) in 1485, when King Richard III was killed, England's battlefields were beginning to change. Cannon-founders had discovered how to make smaller, lighter and more powerful cannons that were quicker to aim and easier to move around the battlefield. The cannon was changing from something that terrorised men and horses by making a lot of noise and smoke to a real weapon that could attack formations of soldiers with devastating effect.

As the gunpowder revolution continued, the ranks of archers who had proved so decisive at battles like Agincourt were soon out of work, replaced by musketeers firing long-barrelled muskets. Pistols were becoming more common, too.

Firearms sealed the fate of the medieval knight: a suit of armour was no defence against a musket ball. Knights disappeared from the battlefield in favour of more mobile, lightly armoured troops.

An early cannon in use at the siege of a castle

Home, sweet home

There is a saying (first recorded in 1628) that an Englishman's home is his castle. For some Englishmen, this was literally true. To protect themselves from attack by rivals, powerful noblemen lived within the thick stone walls of mighty castles. But by the 15th century, cannons were powerful enough to pound their way through castle walls, so there was little point in building defensive castles any more. Instead, noblemen put their money into building grand country houses surrounded by vast gardens.

Going great guns

Cannons transformed war at sea, too. Instead of having to get close enough to an enemy ship to board it, warships could now blast each other to bits from a distance. Bigger and bigger warships were built to carry more guns – and bigger, heavier guns, too. The navies of the great European powers naturally developed new tactics for fighting at sea with these massive guns. Each nation tried to outdo the others in a lethal cat-and-mouse game. British warship gun crews were renowned for their speed. They could load and fire their cannons faster than anyone else, helping to make the English (and, later, British) Royal Navy the most powerful in the world for more than 300 years.

1588: the Royal Navy vs. the Spanish Armada

Natural disasters

Life in the 15th to 18th centuries was nasty, brutal and short enough for most people without nature conspiring against them too. However, England's population was hit by a series of natural disasters during this period, including earthquakes, tsunamis (destructive waves), terrible storms, plagues, famines and even a minor Ice Age.

The period between the 16th and 19th centuries is known as the Little Ice Age. In a succession of cold winters, rivers and canals froze. Sometimes the ice was so thick that 'frost fairs' could be held on the frozen surface. The summers were so short and cold that crop yields fell, and the crops failed altogether in some years. At a time when very little food was imported and people had to survive on food grown in England, this meant disaster. There were famines in England in the 1620s, 1650s and 1690s.

On 6 April 1580, an earthquake ripped through the seabed near Calais, France. The coast of southern England was shaken so violently that a section of the White Cliffs of Dover collapsed, taking part of Dover Castle with it. Buildings were damaged as far away as London, Cambridgeshire and Essex. Powerful aftershocks over the next few days caused more damage.

Twenty-seven years later, on 30 January 1607, a flood described at the time as 'huge and heavy hills of water' moving 'faster than a greyhound can run' swept up the Bristol Channel. It flooded 200 square miles (520 km²) of land and killed 2,000 people. Recent analysis of the sediment carried inshore from the ocean suggests that this was no ordinary flood – it was probably a tsunami, a huge surge of seawater onto the coast caused by an underwater earthquake.

Another tsunami hit Cornwall on 1 November 1755. It was caused by an earthquake off the coast of Portugal. This was one of the most powerful earthquakes in history. Lisbon, the Portuguese capital, was almost totally destroyed and tens of thousands of people died. The massive tsunami unleashed by the earthquake sped away in all directions across the ocean. When it reached Cornwall, it was still 10 feet (3 metres) high. The number of casualties is not recorded, but accounts of the disaster at the time talk about a great loss of life.

Pistols at dawn!

A new import from Italy arrived in England in the 16th century: duelling. The law could right wrongs and punish people, but it couldn't repair a gentleman's honour. That's what duels were intended to do. If a man of repute was insulted, he could challenge his adversary to a duel – a contest with very strict rules.

The two men (and they were nearly always men) appointed friends called 'seconds' to assist them. The seconds were duty-bound to try to settle the argument without a duel, but if they failed, the two opponents appointed a time to meet. They chose a secluded spot where they wouldn't be seen, because duelling was against the law and could be punished with the death penalty. The challenged man chose which weapons they would use. The aim was not necessarily to kill the other man, but to defeat him in face-to-face combat, so a duel could be ended honourably by a wound that made it impossible to continue.

The first duels were fought with swords, but by the late 18th century most duels were fought with pistols. The men stood an agreed distance apart, turned sideways to present as small a target as possible, and fired at each other. Duels were so common that gun-makers created pairs of matched pistols specially for duelling. They had smooth-bore barrels, which made the weapons less accurate than the more common rifled barrels, to give each man a sporting chance of survival.

Duels were most often fought between military officers and noblemen, because the idea of personal honour was particularly important to them. Dr Samuel Johnson (1709–1784), the lexicographer, remarked that 'A man may shoot the man who invades his character, as he may shoot him who attempts to break into his house.'

famous English duels

- **1598:** Playwright Ben Jonson (1572–1637) killed the actor Gabriel Spenser (c.1578–1598) in a duel with swords. No-one knows what caused their disagreement.

- **1772:** Playwright Richard Brinsley Sheridan (1751–1816) fought a sword duel with Captain Thomas Mathews over comments made by Mathews about the woman Sheridan was to marry. Sheridan won, but a further disagreement led to a second duel. Both men broke their swords but fought on, and Sheridan was badly wounded.

- **1789:** HRH Prince Frederick, Duke of York (1763–1827), fought a duel with Lieutenant-Colonel Charles Lennox (1764–1819), who had insulted the prince. Lennox fired first and missed. The prince refused to fire back.

- **1792:** Lady Almeria Braddock and Mrs Elphinstone fought a duel following an argument over Lady Braddock's age. They started with pistols. Neither lady was hurt, so they switched to swords and fought until Mrs Elphinstone was wounded.

- **1798:** William Pitt the Younger (1759–1806), while he was prime minister, fought a duel with another politician, George Tierney (1761–1830). Pitt had accused Tierney of being unpatriotic. Neither man was injured.

fetch the leeches!

If you fell ill in England in earlier centuries, it wasn't simply a matter of popping into a chemist's shop and picking up a reliable brand of painkiller or cough syrup. Medicine at this time was still largely based on ancient beliefs about the human body that science would eventually reject.

Physicians believed in the ancient Greek theory of the four humours. They thought the human body was filled with four fluids, or 'humours': blood, phlegm, black bile and yellow bile. Illness was thought to be the result of these humours getting out of balance. They were brought back into balance by making the patient sweat, bleed, vomit or defecate. If a small amount of blood had to be taken, leeches were used; these wormlike creatures sucked the patient's blood. If more bloodletting was needed, a vein was cut open and the blood was drained into a cup.

A surgical operation was a terrible experience: as no effective anaesthetics were available, surgeons had no option but to cut into patients who were wide awake. The novelist Fanny Burney (1752–1828) underwent a mastectomy in 1811 and described the experience in a letter to her sister; she admits that she screamed uncontrollably throughout. Patients often had to be held down to stop them struggling.

Those who didn't die on the operating table stood a very good chance of dying from an infection afterwards; since the causes of infection were not yet understood, surgeons didn't see any reason to keep themselves, their instruments or their patients clean. Surgery on the battlefield or on board a warship was especially brutal; surgeons often had to amputate an arm or leg as rapidly as possible while the patient screamed in agony.

Fortunately, the scientific revolution of the 17th century led to a better understanding of the human body and how to treat diseases. Instead of merely accepting ancient beliefs, anatomists now studied bodies for themselves to find out how they worked. William Harvey (1578–1657) figured out how blood circulates around the body, pumped by the heart.

To supply doctors and scientists with bodies to study, criminals who had been sentenced to death were also sometimes sentenced to dissection. The need for fresh bodies became so great that body-snatchers made a living by selling bodies stolen from graveyards.

The invention of the microscope at the end of the 16th century enabled scientists to see a whole new world of creatures so small that no-one had known they existed – although it would be a long time before scientists linked these microscopic organisms with disease and infection.

Meanwhile, quacks and tricksters produced their own witch's brews of elixirs, tonics, powders and tablets which were claimed to treat all sorts of illnesses. Parliament finally passed an Apothecaries Act in 1748 to outlaw unqualified medicine-makers.

But all of this is still to come. Let's go back to the early 1400s and resume our history of the English nation. The story is a familiar one: noblemen fighting for the throne.

Battle of Barnet, 1471:
a humiliating defeat for
the Lancastrians in the
Wars of the Roses

CHAPTER ONE

THE WARS OF THE ROSES

When Henry V died in 1422, his 9-month-old son was crowned as Henry VI. A council of noblemen was set up to make decisions for him until he was old enough to rule in his own right.

Henry was a shy and religious man who suffered from bouts of mental disorder. While he was ill, Richard, Duke of York ruled on his behalf. Reluctant to hand power back to Henry, Richard raised an army and attempted to seize the throne. Henry's family, the House of Lancaster, fought back. The two houses were associated with rose emblems – white for the Yorkists and red for the Lancastrians. The prolonged conflict between them eventually became known as the Wars of the Roses.

One house and then the other gained the upper hand. At first, the Yorkists were successful. They captured King Henry, but the fighting continued. This time, the Lancastrians triumphed: Richard was killed at the Battle of Wakefield in 1460, and Henry was briefly returned to power. Even so, Richard of York had been so popular that when he died in 1461 his son was crowned Edward IV. He was the first Yorkist king. He marched north with a huge army and defeated the Lancastrians at Towton in Yorkshire. Henry fled, but was later captured and imprisoned in the Tower of London.

Unfortunately, King Edward fell out with one of his allies, the Earl of Warwick, who changed sides and joined the Lancastrians. Fighting broke out again. Edward fled to Flanders and Henry VI was restored to the throne in 1470. Edward returned to England with an army in 1471 and defeated Warwick, who was killed. King Henry was captured again and sent to the Tower of London, where he died, probably murdered. Henry's son and heir had also died in battle, so Edward IV reigned unchallenged until his death in 1483.

The rivals

Henry VI

Royal house:	House of Lancaster
Reigned:	1422–1461 and 1470–1471
Born:	6 December 1421
Place of birth:	Windsor Castle, Berkshire
Father:	Henry V
Mother:	Catherine of Valois
Died:	21 May 1471
Place of death:	Tower of London

Edward IV

Royal house:	House of York
Reigned:	1461–1470 and 1471–1483
Born:	28 April 1442
Place of birth:	Rouen, Normandy
Father:	Richard Plantagenet, Duke of York
Mother:	Cecily Neville, Duchess of York
Died:	9 April 1483
Place of death:	Westminster

The princes in the Tower

As King Edward IV lay dying, he knew that his 12-year-old son was too young to rule as king, so he named his own brother, Richard Duke of Gloucester, as Protector. Richard was already one of the most powerful men in England. His loyalty to the king had been rewarded with large estates and a series of important titles. When the king died on 9 April 1483, his young son became Edward V, but he would never be crowned. Instead of protecting the king, Richard immediately seized his chance to take the crown for himself. He had the new king taken to the Tower of London, where he was soon joined by his 9-year-old brother, Richard, Duke of York.

The two boys had expected to leave the Tower on 22 June 1483 for Edward's coronation, but they were never seen again. No-one knows what happened to them, but they are thought to have been murdered on the orders of their uncle, Richard of Gloucester. While they were alive, they were a threat to Richard's ambitions. Richard had already had Edward

IV's marriage declared invalid, so his sons had no claim to the throne, but their deaths removed the danger once and for all.

Richard moved quickly to wipe out Edward's closest supporters. Many of them were arrested and executed. Richard's popularity and power, and his own claim to the throne through his parents, made him the obvious choice for king. Just two months after Edward IV died, Richard became king. He was crowned Richard III on 6 July 1483.

The Princes in the Tower

'Deform'd, unfinish'd...'

Richard III is often shown in paintings, and played by actors, as a hunchback with a withered arm. This image of Richard can be traced back to Shakespeare's play *Richard III*. In the play, Richard describes himself as 'deform'd, unfinish'd, sent before my time into this breathing world, scarce half made up'.

Shakespeare based his description on earlier writings by Richard's Tudor enemies. There was a superstitious belief at this time that physical disability was an outward sign of an evil mind, so exaggerated descriptions of Richard's supposed deformities were intended to besmirch his reputation for future generations.

In 2012 it was widely reported that a skeleton showing evidence of scoliosis (curvature of the spine) had been excavated by archaeologists in Leicester. There was said to be good evidence that this skeleton was that of Richard III, but at the time of writing (December 2012) this has not yet been confirmed.

A horse, a horse!

Richard III's enemies were already plotting to replace him as king with the imprisoned Edward V when they learned that the princes in the Tower were dead. They switched their allegiance to Henry Tudor. Henry's claim to the throne came via his mother, who was a descendant of King Edward III. Henry, a Lancastrian, had fled to Brittany in 1471 when his enemy, the Yorkist Edward IV, became king.

The real Richard III

Royal house:	House of York
Reigned:	1483–1485
Born:	2 October 1452
Place of birth:	Fotheringhay Castle, Northants.
Father:	Richard Plantagenet, Duke of York
Mother:	Cecily Neville, Duchess of York
Died:	22 August 1485
Place of death:	Bosworth Field

How they fought in the 15th century

The Wars of the Roses were fought between armies of footsoldiers and knights on horseback.

- Archers were the most numerous soldiers on the battlefield. There were usually at least three times as many archers as other footsoldiers. English and Welsh archers were famed for their prowess with the longbow, a powerful long-range weapon.

- Other footsoldiers were armed with pole-axes, spears, pikes and swords. Pistols and muskets were increasingly common, but they were of limited use because they took a long time to reload.

- Mounted knights still wore full armour at this time. Footsoldiers wore helmets and padded jackets.

Henry's first attempt to return to England, in 1483, failed. His ships had to turn back because of a storm, and his chief ally in England, the Duke of Buckingham, was captured by the king and executed. With support from the French, Henry tried again in 1485. This time he was successful. He landed in Wales and marched towards London with a force of about 5,000 soldiers. Richard met him, with an army numbering more than 10,000, near the small Leicestershire town of Market Bosworth on 22 August 1485. Richard, with the larger army and experience in battle, expected to win.

As the Battle of Bosworth Field raged, Richard spotted Henry moving across the battlefield to a new position. If he could kill Henry, the battle would be won. He set off after Henry with a small group of mounted knights. However, a loyal group of bodyguards protected Henry. Richard's horse became bogged down in the soft ground, forcing him to dismount and fight on foot. In Shakespeare's play, Richard calls for 'a horse, a horse, my kingdom for a horse'. Richard was surrounded by enemy soldiers and killed. He was the last Yorkist king, and the last king of England to die in battle. With their king dead, Richard's army had no reason to fight on. Henry was declared king on the battlefield and presented with Richard's crown.

In his prime: Henry VIII

CHAPTER TWO

A NEW DYNASTY

Henry VII was the first king of a new royal dynasty, the House of Tudor, which would rule England for the next 118 years. Tudor monarchs presided over the rise of the Royal Navy, great voyages of exploration, the growth of England as a world power, the birth of the modern English theatre, the rejection of the Pope's authority and the establishment of a new Church of England. Two of the Tudor monarchs, Henry VIII and Elizabeth I, are among the most famous figures in all of English history.

Your handy guide to the Tudor kings and queens

Monarch	Reigned
Henry VII	1485–1509
Henry VIII	1509–1547
Edward VI	1547–1553
Lady Jane Grey*	10–19 July 1553
Mary I	1553–1558
Elizabeth I	1558–1603

*disputed

The most royal queen?

Was Henry VII's queen, Elizabeth of York, the best-connected English queen ever? She was the daughter, sister, niece, wife and mother of five different English kings:

1. daughter of King Edward IV

2. sister of King Edward V

3. niece of King Richard III

4. wife of King Henry VII

5. mother of King Henry VIII.

Uniting two houses

The new king, Henry VII, was descended from the House of Lancaster. To avoid challenges from the House of York, he tried to unite the two houses by marrying Edward IV's eldest daughter, Elizabeth of York. He also combined the rose emblems of York and Lancaster to form a new royal emblem, the red and white Tudor rose. He rendered the most serious Yorkist supporters powerless by confiscating their land, and rewarded loyal noblemen with honours.

Despite his efforts, he faced a Yorkist challenge within a year of becoming king. Viscount Lovell and two brothers, Humphrey and Thomas Stafford, plotted against Henry, but their revolt was a dismal failure. Lovell had second thoughts and fled to Burgundy. Henry sent troops to deal with the Stafford brothers at Worcester. They claimed sanctuary in the church at Culham near Abingdon, but were dragged out, put on trial for treason and found guilty. Humphrey was executed but Thomas, the younger brother, was pardoned.

Marrying young

People often married at a very young age in Tudor times. Girls could marry at 12 and boys at 14, but they could be promised, or 'contracted', in marriage almost as soon as they were born. Noble and royal families arranged marriages to protect or increase their wealth and power. Sometimes the betrothed couple didn't meet until their wedding day.

Henry VII's mother, Lady Margaret Beaufort, was contracted to marry John de la Pole, the son of the duke of Suffolk, when she was only about seven years old. However, when she became marriageable at the age of 12, King Henry VI chose her as a suitable wife for his half-brother, Edmund Tudor. Margaret was a widow by the time she was 13: Edmund was captured in 1456 during the Wars of the Roses and imprisoned in Carmarthen Castle in Wales, where he died of plague. By then, Margaret was expecting their first child. She gave birth to Henry Tudor, the future King Henry VII, on 28 January 1457 – four months before her 14th birthday.

In Tudor times it wasn't unusual for women to die during childbirth. Margaret Beaufort almost died giving birth to Henry, because her small size at such a young age made the delivery very difficult. Even after a successful birth, a mother could die from infection. The importance of good hygiene had not yet been discovered and there were no effective antiseptics or antibiotics, so an infection that would be dealt with easily today was often a killer in Tudor times.

The first Tudor monarch

Henry VII

Royal house:	House of Tudor
Reigned:	1485–1509
Born:	28 January 1457
Place of birth:	Pembroke Castle, Wales
Father:	Edmund Tudor
Mother:	Lady Margaret Beaufort
Died:	21 April 1509
Place of death:	Richmond Palace, Surrey

Top Tudors

Thomas Wolsey (1473–1530)
A Roman Catholic churchman who became a cardinal and a powerful statesman during Henry VIII's reign. He died of natural causes while on his way to be tried for treason.

Sir Thomas More (1478–1535)
Statesman who was executed for refusing to accept Henry VIII as head of the Church of England after the break with Rome.

Thomas Cromwell (1485–1540)
Statesman and chief minister under Henry VIII, and a supporter of the Reformation; executed for treason.

Thomas Cranmer (1489–1556)
Archbishop of Canterbury during the reigns of Henry VIII, Edward VI and Mary I; a key figure of the Reformation, and a Catholic martyr.

Hans Holbein the Younger (1497–1543)
King's Painter to Henry VIII, noted for his lifelike portraits of Tudor dignitaries.

Sir William Cecil, Lord Burghley (1521–1598)
Secretary of State, Lord High Treasurer and chief advisor to Queen Elizabeth I.

Mary, Queen of Scots (1542–1587)
Deposed queen of Scotland who was imprisoned and eventually executed by Queen Elizabeth I.

Royal pretenders

In 1487, when an Oxford priest called Richard Simon heard rumours that the young Earl of Warwick – a possible claimant to the throne – had died in the Tower of London, he saw an opportunity to be a kingmaker. He chose a boy called Lambert Simnel, the son of an Oxford tradesman, to impersonate Warwick. Simon started a rumour that Warwick had escaped from the Tower. He presented Simnel as Warwick and took him to Ireland, where there was still support for the House of York.

On 24 May 1487, Simnel was crowned in Dublin as Edward VI. He raised an army to invade England. When King Henry learned what was happening, he had the real Earl of Warwick brought from the Tower and shown in public to stop English noblemen from supporting Simnel. It worked in England, but the Irish continued to support the impostor.

Simnel's army landed in England on 5 June 1487, and clashed with Henry's army 11 days later at the Battle of Stoke Field in

Nottinghamshire. The king's army took just three hours to defeat the rebels. Although Simnel was guilty of treason, he was a young lad, only about 12 years old, and Henry could see that he was a puppet in the hands of powerful men. Simnel was therefore pardoned and given a job in the royal kitchen.

Four years later, Henry faced another royal pretender. In 1491, a young boy from Flanders travelled to Ireland with his employer, a silk merchant. The boy's name was Perkin Warbeck. Yorkist supporters thought the young man dressed in fine silk looked like Richard, Duke of York, the younger of the two princes in the Tower. News that the Duke of York might be free spread across Europe. The French king, Charles VIII, invited Warbeck to France in 1492 and welcomed him as a royal prince. Then Warbeck travelled to Flanders, where he met Margaret, Duchess of Burgundy. She introduced him to the most powerful ruler in Europe, the Holy Roman Emperor Maximilian I. Maximilian backed Warbeck and preparations for an invasion of England began.

Henry VII's spies learned of the plotters' plans. When the invasion force arrived at Deal, in Kent, the king's men were waiting for them. Many of the invaders were killed as they landed. Warbeck sensibly stayed on board his ship and sailed away. When he reached Scotland, he was welcomed by the Scottish king, James IV. In September 1496, James and Warbeck invaded Northumberland in the north of England, but they retreated back to Scotland when English troops arrived.

James tired of the young pretender and sent him away. In September 1497, Warbeck arrived in Cornwall, where supporters proclaimed him King Richard IV. They marched on Exeter, but failed to take the city. When Henry VII's men arrived, Warbeck fled to Beaulieu Abbey in Hampshire, where he later surrendered. On 23 November 1499, the 25-year-old Perkin Warbeck was taken from the Tower of London to Tyburn, an infamous execution ground, where he was hanged and beheaded.

An unexpected heir

Henry VII's marriage to Elizabeth of York produced seven children, but only four surivived childhood. Arthur, his eldest son, was expected to become king. However, Arthur died from an unknown illness in 1502, at the age of only 15, and Henry's other son, also called Henry, unexpectedly became heir to the throne. Arthur had married a Spanish princess, Catherine of Aragon, forming an alliance between England and Spain. This alliance was so important that the king negotiated a Papal dispensation for Prince Henry to marry his brother's widow.

When Henry VII died from tuberculosis on 21 April 1509, his 17-year-old son became King Henry VIII. One of the new king's most important jobs was to produce a male heir to inherit the throne and keep the house of Tudor in power. Unfortunately, all of the children from Henry's marriage to Catherine of Aragon died in childhood, except for a daughter, Mary. Henry asked the Pope to annul his marriage to Catherine so that he could marry someone else, but the Pope refused. A lesser king might have obeyed the Pope, but Henry was made of sterner stuff. He broke England's connection with the Catholic Church and declared himself head of the Church in England. When one of Henry's closest advisors, Sir Thomas More, refused to accept Henry as the head of the Church and his new queen, Anne Boleyn, as Henry's lawful wife, he was executed. This period of religious upheaval in England is called the Reformation.

Defender of the faith

The Protestant movement, protesting against some of the teachings of the Catholic Church, began in Germany in the early 1500s. Henry VIII was at first such a loyal supporter of the Catholic Church and opponent of Protestantism that Pope Leo X rewarded him with the title *Fidei Defensor* (Defender of the Faith).

When Henry separated the Church in England from the Catholic Church, the Pope withdrew the title. However, the English Parliament later awarded him the same title, which the British monarch still holds today.

47

An heir of desperation

Henry VIII married six times to satisfy his need for male heirs. His six wives were:

1 Catherine of Aragon (1485–1536)

Married Henry in 1509. Mother of 'Bloody' Queen Mary I. The marriage was annulled in 1533 when Catherine failed to produce a surviving male heir.

2 Anne Boleyn (c.1501–1536)

Married Henry in 1533. Anne produced a daughter, Elizabeth, but no male heir. She was found guilty of high treason and sentenced to death. The usual penalty was to be burned alive, but Henry ordered her to be beheaded. Beheading was usually carried out by axe, but Henry had a swordsman, Jean Rombaud, brought from France to carry out the execution.

3 Jane Seymour (c.1508–1537)

Henry married Jane Seymour in 1536. She finally produced a male heir, Edward, but died of an infection 12 days after the birth.

4 Anne of Cleves (1515–1557)

Henry's chief minister, Thomas Cromwell, urged the king to marry this German noblewoman. Henry sent his court painter, Hans Holbein, to make a portrait of her, but when Henry finally met her, he was disappointed. The marriage went ahead in 1540 but was annulled after just six months.

5 Catherine Howard (c.1521–1542)

Cousin to Anne Boleyn and lady-in-waiting to Anne of Cleves, Catherine was 30 years younger than the 49-year-old king when they married in 1540. Within a few months of the marriage, there were rumours that she had been unfaithful to the king. She was found guilty of treason and executed.

6 Catherine Parr (1512–1548)

Catherine Parr had been married and widowed twice before she married Henry VIII in 1543. She published the first book written by an English queen in her own name. She outlived Henry and married for a fourth time.

The Dissolution of the Monasteries

By the 1530s, Henry VIII was short of money. Looking enviously at wealthy monasteries up and down the country, he ordered that all the money they sent to Rome should be paid to him instead. Then he set about closing the monasteries down and taking everything they owned. Their gold and silver were melted down, their stained-glass windows were smashed and their libraries were destroyed. Other property was sold and most of the land was sold or rented out. Even the bricks and stone from some of the buildings were taken away to be reused, so some monasteries were quickly reduced to ruins. In four years, from 1536, more than 800 monasteries and other religious buildings were closed, or 'dissolved'. The Dissolution of the Monasteries has been called the greatest act of vandalism in English history. It made Henry very rich and even more powerful.

When the Scots refused to break with Rome, Henry sent an army north to 'persuade' them. The Scots were defeated at the battle of Solway Moss. The Scottish king, James V, died soon afterwards and his daughter inherited the throne as Mary, Queen of Scots. We'll hear more of her later...

Large as life
Henry VIII

Royal house:	House of Tudor
Reigned:	1509–1547
Born:	28 June 1491
Place of birth:	Greenwich Palace
Father:	King Henry VII
Mother:	Elizabeth of York
Died:	28 January 1547
Place of death:	Palace of Whitehall

51

Building a navy

Having abandoned the Catholic Church, Henry feared that England's enemies, France and Spain, might invade England to put a Catholic monarch on the throne. An invasion force would have to be landed by ship, so Henry set about building a chain of coastal forts and a powerful navy to protect the country and its vital sea routes.

One of Henry's favourite warships was the *Mary Rose*. One of the biggest warships of its time, it was launched in 1511 and fought in several wars. In 1536 it was rebuilt: extra guns were added and the weight of the ship increased massively.

In 1545, Henry learned that the French were preparing to invade England. In July, a French force sailed to attack Portsmouth, a major naval base on England's south coast. Henry's fleet sailed into action but, as the *Mary Rose* turned towards the enemy, it heeled over. Water poured in through its open gun ports. With the king watching from the shore, the ship quickly sank. Most of the crew were trapped under the heavy netting which was tied over the deck to stop enemy soldiers from boarding the ship. Of the 400 crewmen on board, only about 35 survived.

The ship rammed itself into the muddy seabed on its side. Over the centuries, one half of the hull rotted away, but the half that was buried in the mud was preserved. It was raised to the surface in 1982. Tens of thousands of items used by the crew were found, together with about 200 skeletons. The remains of the ship can be seen today at Portsmouth Historic Dockyard.

The loss of the
Mary Rose

How the other half lived

How they dressed in Tudor times

Tudor people couldn't wear whatever they liked. Sumptuary laws (laws governing expenditure) laid down what everyone was allowed to wear. The rules were supposed to protect people from spending more than they could afford, but actually they were to keep people in their place. Royalty and noblemen didn't want lower-class merchants dressing better than them! The sumptuary laws included:

- **Purple silk and sable fur:** To be worn only by the king and queen and their family.

- **Crimson or scarlet velvet:** To be worn only by dukes, marquises and earls.

- **Tinselled cloth (woven with gold or silver thread):** To be worn only by dukes, marquises, earls and their children, viscounts, barons, knights of the Garter and members of the Privy Council.

Lower-class people had to wear clothes made of wool, linen or sheepskin. The only permitted colours were brown, beige, yellow, orange, russet, green and pale blue.

A sporting king

When Henry VIII was a young man, he was fit, healthy and athletic. He was fond of hunting and all sorts of sports, including tennis, bowls, wrestling, falconry and jousting. He even had a tennis court built at one of his favourite palaces, Hampton Court.

Some sports that are illegal today were popular in Tudor times. One of these was cockfighting. Two cockerels were made to fight each other, while onlookers gambled on which bird would win. Henry had a cockpit built at Whitehall Palace in London. Most of the palace burned down in the 17th century. Today, 10 Downing Street, where the British prime minister lives and works, stands on the land where Henry VIII built his cockpit.

Henry is said to have competed fearlessly in jousting contests, in which two knights on horseback galloped towards each other with long lances, each trying to unseat the other. Though the knights wore armour and carried shields, it was a very dangerous sport and injuries were common.

On 24 January 1536, Henry suffered a serious accident in a jousting contest at Greenwich Palace. The 44-year-old king was thrown from his horse, which then fell on him. He was unconscious for two hours. He recovered, but his injuries caused problems with his legs that troubled him for the rest of his life. He may also have suffered a brain injury, because his personality is said to have changed after the accident; the sporty, happy and generous Henry now became known for his anger and cruelty.

Jousting: the extreme sport of kings

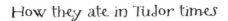

How the other half lived

How they ate in Tudor times

Wealthy Tudors ate a completely different diet from poor people.

- **Meat:** The rich could afford to eat all sorts of meat, including deer, boar, rabbit, hare, beef, mutton, lamb, pork and fowls. Only noblemen were allowed to hunt deer and boar. Poor people who hunted illegally could be executed. They ate meat from animals they could raise or catch lawfully, including chickens and rabbits.

- **Fish:** Fish was an important food for the rich. Landowners and monasteries often farmed their own fish in huge ponds.

- **Vegetables:** Rich people ate very few vegetables, because these were seen as peasant food. Potatoes didn't arrive in England until the reign of Elizabeth I.

- **Dairy:** Milk, butter and eggs were peasant food, eaten and drunk mainly by the poor.

- **Bread:** Eaten by everyone, rich and poor.

Tudor people avoided drinking water, because it could be polluted and might cause fatal diseases. Instead, they drank wine or ale, which was safer. Poor people drank ale, or cider made from apples or pears. Tea and coffee did not arrive in England until the mid-17th century.

Weight a minute!

Henry VIII ate and drank so much and was so inactive because of ill health that his weight soared to nearly 400 lb, or 28½ stone (about 180 kg).

His first suit of armour, made when he was an active young man, had a 34 in. (86 cm) waist. His last suit of armour had to be made with a 60 in. (152 cm) waist

Short reigns

King Henry VIII died on 28 January 1547, at the age of 55. His death was probably hastened by his enormous weight and poor health. He had reigned for almost 38 years, but the next three English monarchs together managed less than 12 years on the throne. One of them, Lady Jane Grey, reigned for only nine days.

Henry was succeeded by his only son. The boy was crowned Edward VI at the age of nine; because of his young age, a council of noblemen ruled on his behalf. He was the first English monarch who was brought up as a Protestant. Reform of the Church of England, to rid it of Catholic practices, continued during his reign. For example, English replaced Latin in church services. When Edward fell ill at the beginning of 1553, he gave some thought to who might succeed him if he died. He didn't want his Catholic half-sister, Mary, to become queen, because she would reverse his religious reforms. He named his 16-year-old cousin Lady Jane Grey as his successor shortly before he died on 6 July 1553.

Jane reigned for only nine days before senior noblemen decided that Mary had the strongest claim to the throne after all. Mary was proclaimed queen and Jane was charged with high treason. She was found guilty and beheaded at the Tower of London. As soon as Mary became queen, she made the Pope the head of the English Church again, freed imprisoned Catholics and reversed Protestant reforms. During her reign, she had hundreds of Protestants burned at the stake, earning her the nickname 'Bloody Mary'. Hundreds more Protestants left the country to escape execution. Mary urgently needed to produce a male heir to stop her Protestant half-sister, Elizabeth, from becoming queen after her. She married Prince Philip of Spain (the future King Philip II), but was unable to have any children. When she died in 1558, Elizabeth succeeded her.

The Virgin Queen

Elizabeth was known as the Virgin Queen, because she never married. But she was pursued by men and enjoyed their attention. One of these was Robert Dudley, later the Earl of Leicester. When Dudley's wife, Amy Robsart, died in suspicious circumstances, there were rumours that Dudley had killed her so he could marry the Queen – but when he secretly married someone else, Elizabeth was furious. She banished him from court and never forgave him.

Good Queen Bess

Royal house: House of Tudor
Reigned: 1558–1603
Born: 7 September 1533
Place of birth: Greenwich Palace
Father: King Henry VIII
Mother: Anne Boleyn
Died: 24 March 1603
Place of death: Richmond Palace

facing the world

Queen Elizabeth wore thick white make-up to cover scarring caused by smallpox, which she suffered from in 1562. The make-up contained toxic lead.

flushed with success

Elizabeth was the first English monarch to have a flushing toilet.

One of her godsons, John Harington, built the convenience for his house at Kelston, near Bath. The queen was so impressed by it that he built another one for her. It didn't catch on, though, because it was noisy, smelly and needed a running water supply, which few houses had. Harington's treatise about his new invention contained satirical remarks which led to his banishment from court.

Robert Devereux, Earl of Essex, became a favourite of the Queen, but he had a habit of disobeying her orders. Elizabeth tired of him after he led an unsuccessful military campaign in Ireland. When he raised an equally unsuccessful rebellion against the government, he was found guilty of treason and beheaded in 1601.

Another favourite, Sir Walter Raleigh, made the same mistake as Dudley: he secretly married one of the Queen's maids. When Elizabeth found out, she jailed the couple.

Elizabeth made visits, called 'progresses', to different parts of England so that her people could see her. The arts, especially the theatre, flourished during her reign. She made the monarchy stronger and more popular than ever.

Eminent Elizabethans

Sir Francis Walsingham (c.1532–1590)
Queen Elizabeth's spymaster, who also oversaw the kingdom's domestic, foreign and religious policies.

Sir Philip Sidney (1554–1586)
A prominent courtier, soldier, diplomat and writer, known for his chivalry.

Sir Francis Drake (1540–1596)
A legendary sailor and privateer who repeatedly attacked Spanish shipping, took part in the sea battle with the Spanish Armada and made the second round-the-world voyage.

Sir Francis Bacon (1561–1626)
A philosopher, scientist, politician and writer who died from pneumonia caused by his research into preserving meat by freezing.

Christopher Marlowe (1564–1593)
A poet and playwright who may also have been a government spy. William Shakespeare is said to have been inspired by Marlowe.

William Shakespeare (1564–1616)
A poet and playwright who is widely recognised as the greatest-ever writer in the English language.

Mary, Queen of Scots

Mary, Queen of Scots was the great-niece of Henry VIII, so she had some claim to the English throne. Some English Catholics hoped she might replace Elizabeth and make England a Catholic country again.

Henry VIII wanted Mary to marry his son, Edward, in order to unite Scotland and England, but instead she married the Dauphin (the eldest son of the French king). He became King Francis II of France in 1559, but reigned for only a year and a half before dying at the age of 16.

After the French king's death, Mary returned to Scotland. She discovered that it was no longer the Catholic country she had left as a child. Scottish Protestants did not welcome the return of a Catholic queen. In 1565 she married an English-born nobleman, Lord Darnley. The marriage was not a happy union. Darnley was jealous of his wife's friendship with an Italian-born court musician, David Rizzio, who became her secretary.

In 1566, Darnley and a band of men overpowered the royal guards at Holyrood Palace in Edinburgh and burst into the Queen's chambers, where they found Rizzio and killed him in front of the queen.

Darnley himself died a year later in suspicious circumstances. Gunpowder exploded under his room and he was found dead outside, but he was not killed by the explosion – he had been strangled!

The Auld Alliance

Scotland and France had long ago formed an alliance to protect each other from the English. If either country was attacked by England, the other promised to come to its aid. It was called the Auld (old) Alliance and it lasted from the 13th century to the 16th century.

Mary caused a scandal by marrying the man accused of Darnley's murder, the Earl of Bothwell. She quickly fell out of favour with the nobility and ordinary people. She abdicated (gave up the throne) and fled to England.

Once Mary was in England, she was a more serious threat to Queen Elizabeth. Elizabeth's advisors urged her to execute Mary. They uncovered plot after plot aimed at removing Elizabeth from the throne and replacing her with Mary. Elizabeth was reluctant to execute Mary, but kept her locked up. Sir Francis Walsingham, Elizabeth's spymaster, finally convinced the Queen that Mary was plotting against her. Mary and several conspirators were put on trial for treason and found guilty. The conspirators met a very grisly end: they were hanged, drawn and quartered. Then, on 8 February 1587, Mary herself was beheaded at Fotheringay Castle in Northamptonshire.

Death mask of Mary, Queen of Scots

The Spanish Armada

In the 1580s the king of Spain, Philip II – the widower of Queen Mary of England – was trying to force the Spanish Netherlands (Holland and Belgium today) to accept Catholicism, but many of the people preferred to be Protestant. England's support for these Protestants angered Philip. English attacks on Spanish ships were also costing Spain a great deal of money in sunken ships and stolen cargoes. Finally, Philip decided to put an end to these problems by invading England.

He planned to send a great Armada (fleet of warships) to collect an army from Holland and take them to England. When English spies learned of Philip's plan, the navy attacked the Spanish ports of Cádiz and Corunna (La Coruña), where the Armada was gathering. The English fleet under Sir Francis Drake destroyed dozens of ships, delaying the Armada for a year. The action was described at the time as 'singeing the King of Spain's beard'.

In July 1588, the Armada set sail for England under the command of the Duke of Medina

Sidonia. The English fleet, under Lord Howard of Effingham and his Vice-Admiral, Sir Francis Drake, was waiting for them. Elizabeth rallied her troops at Tilbury in Essex with a speech that included the famous line, 'I know I have the body of a weak and feeble woman, but I have the heart and stomach of a king, and a king of England, too.'

When the Spanish ships sheltered in Calais, the English sent burning ships amongst them to make them scatter. On 8 August 1588, the two fleets met at the Battle of Gravelines, near Calais. The English gained the upper hand, but didn't totally defeat the Armada – the weather took care of that.

Before the Spanish ships could pick up their invasion army, strong winds blew them north. They had to sail all the way round Scotland and Ireland to return to Spain. Many of the ships were wrecked on the way. Two more armadas were sent in 1596 and 1597, but they met a similar fate.

The play's the thing

Queen Elizabeth I's reign was a golden age for the theatre in England. A young actor and playwright called William Shakespeare had the good fortune to be working at a time when the first playhouses (theatres) were being built in London. The first permanent London playhouse, called The Theatre, opened in 1576. Until then, plays had been performed by travelling actors in palaces, grand houses, public buildings and inn-yards. The first theatres proved to be very popular with the public. Rival theatres opened with their own groups of actors. Shakespeare belonged to one of the leading groups, the Lord Chamberlain's Men. In 1599, having fallen out with their previous landlord, they built a new theatre of their own: The Globe.

The Globe theatre

The audience at the Globe paid a penny to stand and watch a play, another penny for a seat, and a third penny if they wanted a cushion. It was illegal for women to act on the stage, so women's parts were played by boys.

Nearly 40 of Shakespeare's plays have survived to the present day, along with 154 sonnets (poems of 14 lines) and several longer poems. He is widely thought of as the greatest English dramatist who ever lived. At the end of his working life, in about 1613, he retired to the town of his birth, Stratford-upon-Avon in Warwickshire, where he died in 1616 at the age of 52. He was survived by his wife, Anne, and two daughters.

Pirates and privateers

The great powers of Europe established colonies in the Americas and the Far East from the 15th century onwards. As their empires grew, trade increased, and so did piracy. Pirates patrolled the sea routes, attacking ships and stealing their cargoes.

There were two types of pirates. Privateers had government backing to attack the shipping of rival countries, especially during wartime. Ordinary pirates had no government backing; they attacked whoever they wished. They were hunted by the navy and, if they were caught, they could expect to be executed.

English pirates cruised the Caribbean looking for Spanish ships carrying gold and silver from the Americas to Spain. Famous explorers and naval officers of the Elizabethan age were also privateers, including Sir Francis Drake, Sir Walter Raleigh and Sir Martin Frobisher. Drake caused the Spanish so much trouble that they called him *El Draque* (The Dragon). These privateers were heroes to the English but common pirates to their enemies.

Elizabethan piracy

The legend of Drake's Drum

Drake carried a large drum with him on his great voyages of exploration. Shortly before he died of dysentery off the coast of Panama in 1596, he ordered his drum to be taken to his family home, Buckland Abbey in Devon. It is still there today. He said that if England was ever in danger again, someone should beat the drum and he would come back from the dead to defend the country.

How they lived and died
in Tudor England

For many in Tudor England, life could be short and brutal.

- **Population:** The population of England was 3–4 million. Most lived in villages and worked in farming. The capital, London, was by far the biggest city: between 1500 and 1600 its population grew from about 50,000 to 200,000. Few other towns had a population of more than 5,000.

- **Homes:** While merchants and noblemen lived in large houses with numerous servants, half of the population had only just enough food and shelter to survive. Their homes had no water supply or toilets. They were heated by open fires and lit by candles.

- **Disease:** Towns were smelly, because people threw their rubbish into the street. Conditions were so overcrowded that diseases spread quickly. Smallpox, cholera, typhus, tuberculosis and dysentery were common.

- **Life expectancy:** Poor diet and bad health meant that people didn't live as long in the Tudor age as they do today. While some people lived to their 70s or even into their 80s, the average lifespan was only about 35 years, compared to more than 80 years today.

A 17th-century supergun:
Roaring Meg, a mortar used
by the Roundheads at the
siege of Goodrich Castle, 1646

CAVALIERS AND ROUNDHEADS

The Stuart monarchs ruled England during one of the most turbulent times in the country's history. England was plunged into a civil war that ended with the unthinkable – the execution of the king. An unstoppable plague swept through the population. England's capital city was almost destroyed by a great fire. Trouble flared up in Scotland and Ireland. But this was also a time of exploration and discovery: some of England's greatest scientists lived and worked during this time.

Your handy guide to the Stuart kings and queens of England (and Great Britain)

	Reigned
James I*	1603–1625
Charles I	1625–1649
Charles II	1649–1685
James II**	1685–1688
Mary II***	1689–1694
Anne	1702–1714

* also James VI of Scotland, 1567–1625.
** James VII of Scotland.
***Ruled jointly with her husband, William III (r.1689–1702).

The first of the Stuarts
James I

Royal house:	House of Stuart
Reigned:	1603–1625
Born:	19 June 1566
Place of birth:	Edinburgh Castle
Father:	Henry Stuart, Lord Darnley
Mother:	Mary, Queen of Scots
Died:	27 March 1625
Place of death:	Theobalds House, Cheshunt, Herts.

The Union of Crowns

Queen Elizabeth I died childless in 1603, ending the Tudor Age. Who would succeed her? Mary, Queen of Scots was her cousin, so Mary's son, the Protestant King James VI of Scotland, had a claim to the English throne. He was proclaimed king of England on the very day Elizabeth died, and ushered in the Stuart era in England. All four countries of the British Isles – England, Wales, Scotland and Ireland – had the same monarch for the first time.

James quickly made himself unpopular. He behaved harshly towards both Protestants and Catholics. He had a strong belief in the Divine Right of Kings – the idea that kings were appointed by God – so he felt that no-one, not even Parliament, had the right to question his decisions.

Parliament angered him by refusing his wish to be called the king of Great Britain. It also refused to unite England and Scotland under the same Parliament and to impose higher taxes, so James was always short of money. He became so frustrated that he dissolved Parliament and governed on his own.

A new flag

Although England and Scotland remained separate countries with their own national flags (the English flag was the Cross of St George and the Scots flew St Andrew's Cross), James decided to combine the two in a new royal flag, the 'King's Colours'. This became the national flag of Great Britain when England and Scotland were finally united in 1707. The flag of Ireland, St Patrick's cross, was added in 1801 to produce the Union Flag, or Union Jack, still in use today.

St George   St Andrew   St Patrick

The King's Bible

One of the first things James did when he became king of England was to order the production of a new English translation of the Bible. There had been English Bibles since the 15th century, but they were controversial and based on unreliable sources.

The Bible was divided into six parts and a team of translators and Bible scholars was put to work on each part. The new translation took four years to complete; then a committee went through the translation and checked it. Finally, the new Bible was printed in 1611. It enabled large numbers of English men and women to read the Bible in their own language.

The King James Bible, also known as the Authorised Version, became the standard Bible for English-speaking Protestants everywhere. It is so beautifully written that it has remained popular to the present day. It has been in print, continuously, for the past 400 years and is the all-time best-selling book in the English language.

Gunpowder, treason and plot

On the night of 4 November 1605, the day before James was due to open a new session of Parliament, soldiers searched the cellars underneath the Houses of Parliament. There they found a man called Guy Fawkes and 36 barrels of gunpowder. It was enough to reduce Parliament to rubble and kill everyone inside it, including the King. Fawkes was one of a dozen or so conspirators whose aim was to kill the King and replace him with his daughter, the Catholic Princess Elizabeth.

Plots are supposed to be secret, but James knew about this one. More than a week earlier, Lord Monteagle had received an anonymous letter warning him to stay away from Parliament on 5 November. It was passed on to the King. Surprisingly, although the conspirators knew their plot had been discovered, they still went ahead.

Fawkes admitted that he planned to kill the King, but claimed he had acted alone. His interrogators didn't believe him, because they already knew the names of several of the plotters. James gave permission for Fawkes to be tortured. He held out for two days before telling everything he knew.

Meanwhile, most of the plotters had fled to Holbeche House in Staffordshire, where they prepared to defend themselves. When they discovered that their gunpowder was damp, they tried to dry it out in front of a fire. A spark landed on it and it exploded, injuring several men. Hundreds of soldiers arrived and surrounded the house. In the attack that followed, four plotters were arrested; the others were killed or escaped. The surviving plotters were taken to the Tower of London for questioning. Then they were put on trial and found guilty of treason.

The penalty was death – a very gruesome death. Eight men were hanged in public, then cut down while still alive and disembowelled. Then their bodies were cut into quarters. Guy Fawkes managed to cheat the executioner: when the noose was placed around his neck, he jumped from the gallows and broke his neck, giving himself a quick death.

The Pilgrim fathers

Although a Protestant himself, James was tolerant of law-abiding Catholics. But life in England in the early 1600s could be difficult for the extreme Protestants known as Puritans. In 1620, a group of Puritans gave up on England and set sail for the New World in a ship called the *Mayflower*. These 'Pilgrims' or 'Pilgrim Fathers', as they are known, called their American colony New England.

The Mayflower sets sail for the New World

Hunting witches

In the 1600s, people still believed in the existence of witches. Waves of witch-hunting had swept across Europe since ancient times. In 1487, a notorious book called *Malleus Maleficarum* (The Hammer of the Witches) was published in Germany. It explained how to find witches and told judges how to convict them in court. Nearly all of the people accused of practising witchcraft were women. Once accused, they faced torture to make them confess and, if found guilty in court, they could expect to be executed by hanging or being burned at the stake.

Witch-hunting erupted in England during James I's reign. (James himself had published a book on the subject in 1597.) One witch-hunter, Matthew Hopkins, was infamous. Towns and villages hired him to find the witches in their midst, get confessions from them and have them executed. In the 1640s he condemned more than 200 unfortunate victims to death.

Me? I'm just a little old lady who loves cats.

Decline and death

The end of James I's reign was blighted by his failing health. He suffered from arthritis, gout, kidney stones, fainting fits and dysentery – and he lost his teeth. At the beginning of 1625 he fell seriously ill and suffered a stroke. In his weakened state, an attack of dysentery proved too much for him. He died on March 27.

Although James had been unpopular as king, he was widely mourned when he died, because the country had enjoyed a long period of peace during his reign. He had brought the long-running Anglo-Spanish War (1585–1604) to an end and signed a peace treaty with Spain that held until his death. As a gesture of goodwill to the Spanish, James had ordered Sir Walter Raleigh to be executed after Raleigh had enraged the Spanish by raiding one of its colonies in the Americas.

James and his wife, Anne of Denmark, had seven children, but only three of them lived to their teens and beyond. One of them, Charles, succeeded James as King Charles I, the second Stuart monarch.

The first Charles

King Charles I started where his father had left off – arguing with Parliament and dissolving it when it disagreed with him. As Charles was Catholic, his despotic rule outraged the most extreme Protestants, the Puritans. He tried to force his wishes on Scotland, but failed. However, his Scottish campaign left him very short of money. He needed money to fight wars in Europe, so he was forced to recall Parliament, as he could not raise sufficient taxes without their consent. The new parliament demanded changes, including a law stopping him from dissolving Parliament whenever he wished.

Charles I

Royal house:	House of Stuart
Reigned:	1625–1649
Born:	19 November 1600
Place of birth:	Dunfermline Palace, Scotland
Father:	King James I and VI
Mother:	Anne of Denmark
Died:	30 January 1649
Place of death:	Whitehall, London

Charles accused some of the politicians of treason. In 1642, he went to Parliament to arrest them, but the men had been warned and fled. Parliamentarians were outraged by the king's actions and he was angry that they had outwitted him. He raised an army and declared war on the Parliamentarians, who raised their own army. This was war – usually known as the English Civil War, though the fighting extended to Scotland and Ireland as well. An MP called Oliver Cromwell joined the army and quickly rose through the ranks.

Hair today, gone tomorrow

The two sides in the English Civil War were nicknamed Cavaliers and Roundheads. The King's supporters, or Royalists, wore fashionable wigs of long curly hair. The Parliamentarians showed that they were not supporters of the King by cutting their hair short and not wearing wigs. The Royalists called them Roundheads as a term of abuse. In return, the Parliamentarians called the Royalists Cavaliers (literally 'horsemen' or 'gentlemen'), implying that they were frivolous and ungodly.

Civil War battles

There were dozens of battles during the English Civil War, but three of them were especially important: Edgehill, Marston Moor and Naseby.

- **Edgehill, 23 October 1642:** The first battle of the war. As the King and his army marched from Shrewsbury to London, they met the enemy near Edge Hill in Warwickshire. Of the 27,000 soldiers who took part, about 500 on each side were killed and 1,500 wounded. The battle was indecisive.

- **Marston Moor, 2 July 1644:** As 40,000 soldiers took up positions for battle near Long Marston in North Yorkshire, the Parliamentarians launched a surprise attack and won. The Royalists suffered heavy losses: around 4,000 dead, compared to only 300 Parliamentarians. This battle ended Royalist control of northern England.

- **Naseby, 14 June 1645:** The rival armies faced each other near Naseby in Northamptonshire. They seemed evenly matched, but the Parliamentarians, commanded by Thomas Fairfax and Oliver Cromwell, utterly destroyed the Royalist army, leading to victory in the war the following year.

Oliver Cromwell

While there were many important Parliamentarians and military commanders during the English Civil War, one name stands out from all the rest: Oliver Cromwell.

Cromwell was a Member of Parliament during the time when relations between the King and Parliament were breaking down. He was a very religious man, an anti-Catholic who felt that the Reformation had not gone far enough. When the Civil War began, he joined the Parliamentarian army. Although he had almost no previous military experience, he was a successful soldier and quickly earned promotion. When the Parliamentarians formed a new army of well-trained professional troops called the New Model Army in 1645, Cromwell was appointed its second-in-command.

He would soon become even more powerful, but first there was the matter of what to do with the King. He had been handed over to the Parliamentarians by a Scottish army that was sheltering him.

To kill a king

In England in the 1600s, it was unthinkable that anyone might harm a figure as powerful as the King. When Charles I was arrested and put on trial for treason – which could result in his execution if found guilty – the shock in the country can scarcely be imagined. The trial began on 20 January 1649, at Westminster Hall in London. The king was accused of betraying his own country and being responsible for all the bloodshed that resulted. Charles refused to recognise the court. He said, 'I would know by what power I am called hither.' After a trial lasting a week, he was found guilty and sentenced to death.

On 30 January 1649, King Charles I walked out onto a public scaffold built next to the Banqueting House in London and kneeled in front of his executioner. To stop himself from shivering on the cold morning – which might be mistaken for shaking with fear – he had asked for an extra shirt. As the axe fell and the King died, there was no cheering. People feared what might happen next.

England was now governed by Parliament instead of a monarch. Royalists held out the hope of putting Charles I's son, also called Charles, on the throne. However, the young heir was forced to flee to France.

Dealing with Ireland

Although the Royalists were defeated in England, there was still support for them in Ireland. Cromwell, who was anti-royal as well as anti-Catholic, went to Ireland in 1649 to deal with the Irish Royalists. His army put down any resistance or dissent with great brutality. When the town of Drogheda was captured, he had 3,500 Royalist soldiers, armed civilians and even priests killed. Another 3,500 troops and civilians were killed at the Siege of Wexford when Cromwell's troops burst into the town. There were more massacres, but Cromwell firmly believed he was carrying out God's will. With the Irish rebellion put down, Cromwell returned to England to deal with the news that Charles I's son had landed in Scotland and had been proclaimed King Charles II.

Invading Scotland

Cromwell led an invasion force into Scotland in 1650. At first, the Scottish got the better of Cromwell's troops and almost defeated them. Cromwell retreated from Edinburgh to Dunbar, chased by the Scots. He managed to reorganise his forces and attack again, snatching victory from the jaws of defeat. About 4,000 Scottish soldiers were killed and another 10,000 were taken prisoner. Cromwell returned to Edinburgh and took the city. After this extraordinary reversal of fortune, Cromwell was more convinced than ever that God was on his side.

In desperation, a Scottish force invaded England and headed straight for London. Cromwell's army caught up with them at Worcester and crushed them. Young Charles escaped and fled to Europe.

Lord Protector

After Charles I's execution, England became a Commonwealth ruled by a Council of State. However, Oliver Cromwell seized power for himself in 1653 and ruled as Lord Protector. He argued with Parliament as much as Charles I had. In 1658, he fell ill with malaria and died on 3 September at the age of 59. His son, Richard, became Lord Protector after him, but Richard was not as powerful as his father. He was nicknamed 'Tumbledown Dick'. He was forced to recall Parliament, which voted to abolish the Protectorate in 1659. Charles I's son was invited back to England. He rejected the Divine Right of Kings and agreed to accept the advice of Parliament. He was crowned Charles II in 1660. England had a king again after a gap, or interregnum, of 11 years.

On 30 January 1661, exactly 12 years after Charles I's execution, Oliver Cromwell's body was dug up and 'executed'. His head was stuck on a pole outside Westminster Hall, where Charles I had faced trial, where it remained until 1685.

Charles II

Royal house: House of Stuart
Reigned: 1660–1685
Born: 29 May 1630
Place of birth: St James's Palace, London
Father: Charles I
Mother: Henrietta Maria of France
Died: 6 February 1685
Place of death: Whitehall Palace, London

Dull Puritans

Cromwell imposed Puritan values on England.
He closed inns and theatres, and banned
certain sports, games and maypole dancing.
Even Christmas dinner and seasonal festivities
were banned. Life in England for most people
became rather dull under the Puritans.

A very merry monarch

When Charles II entered London, he was greeted by cheering crowds who were tired of life under the Puritans. Charles II enjoyed life to the full, earning the nickname the 'merry monarch'.

Restoration fashions

Fashion changed when Charles II came to the throne. The sombre, plain clothing of the Puritan years was thrown off and replaced with bright colours, ribbons and lace – and that was just the men!

- **Clothes:** Charles started a new fashion in men's clothes. He introduced the three-piece suit to England. The waistcoat was inspired by clothes seen by European travellers in Persia (now Iran). Women wore dresses with plunging necklines that the Puritans would not have approved of.

- **Hats:** Men wore tall hats over long wigs and women wore lace headdresses over tightly curled hair.

The Dutch wars

While England was at peace with itself after the long years of civil war and Puritan domination, it was not at peace with its neighbours. The English and Dutch had gone to war with each other during Cromwell's time over competition for overseas trade. The war ended with an English victory and peace treaty, but England had not been able to take control of the valuable Dutch sea-trade routes.

By 1664, the English felt confident enough to take on the Dutch again. English forces attacked Dutch colonies in Africa and North America. The two countries were soon at war. In 1667, with the English desperately short of money for the navy, the Dutch made a daring and successful attack on the English fleet in the River Medway in Kent. The English willingly signed a peace treaty to avoid suffering further humiliation.

In 1672, England joined forces with France and attacked the Dutch yet again. This time, Parliament forced the king to abandon the war because the cost was ruinous.

Coffeehouses

During the 17th century, a new drink became popular in England: coffee. People drank it in a new type of shop, the coffeehouse. The first coffeehouses in England opened in the 1650s. By 1675, there were more than 3,000.

Charles II was suspicious of coffeehouses, because he thought they were places where people could meet to spread rumours and hatch plots. He tried to close them down, but there was such an outcry that he had to give in and let them stay open. They were places where – rarely for that time – people from different social classes could meet and mix. Most of the customers in a coffeehouse were men. Women were allowed in, but coffeehouses were not thought to be fitting places for respectable women to go.

As international trade grew in Charles II's England, coffeehouses quickly became places where merchants and ship owners met to do business deals.

The trade triangle

The most profitable sea-trade in the 17th century was a three-way trade route called the 'trade triangle'. Ships took goods and materials from England to sell in West Africa. When they were unloaded, the ships took on a new cargo, a human cargo: slaves. The slaves were transported across the Atlantic ocean to work on plantations in the Americas. Those slaves who managed to survive the gruelling 6–8 week voyage were unloaded and replaced with the produce of the plantations, including sugar and tobacco, for the return journey to England.

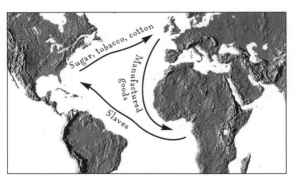

The slave-trade triangle

The Great Plague

A terrible disease called the plague had broken out in England several times since the 14th century, but an outbreak in 1665 was the worst since the Black Death of 1348. Charles II banned trade with the Netherlands after an outbreak of plague there in 1663, but this failed to stop the disease spreading to England. It began in London in February 1665, and spread rapidly during the hot summer. No-one knew what caused it. Some thought it might be carried by dogs and cats, so 40,000 dogs and 200,000 cats were killed. This actually made the outbreak worse, since the plague was carried by fleas living on rats. With fewer dogs and cats to kill the rats, the rat and flea population soared.

The plague worsened until the cold winter weather started killing the rats and the epidemic finally eased. When people returned to the capital, one in five Londoners had died – about 100,000 people. There were so many victims that carts toured the city at night collecting the dead. The bodies were taken away and buried in mass graves.

Plague rhyme

A popular children's rhyme at the time of the plague was 'Ring a ring o' roses':

> Ring a ring o' roses,
> A pocket full of posies.
> Atishoo! Atishoo!
> We all fall down.

The 'ring o' roses' described the red rash that plague victims had, and 'Atishoo' refers to the sneezing of people falling ill with the plague, before they 'fell down' and died.

Urban myth

It is sometimes said that the town of Gravesend in Kent was so named because it was where the mass graves of plague victims from London ended, or where the bodies of plague victims thrown into the River Thames washed up. It's a good story, but it isn't true. The name of the town dates back to at least 1100, more than 500 years before the 1665 plague.

Plague doctors

People who were unlucky enough to catch the plague were shut in their homes so they couldn't infect anyone else. A red cross was painted on their door, with the words 'Lord have mercy on us.' The doctors who tried to treat plague victims looked very alarming. They wore an ankle-length coat, gloves, boots, a wide-brimmed hat and a face mask in the shape of a bird's beak. They thought plague might be spread by bad smells in the air, so the bird's beak was filled with strong-smelling flowers and herbs to keep the bad smells out.

A visit from the plague doctor

The Great fire of London

In 1666, London suffered a terrible disaster that destroyed more than three-quarters of the city. In the early hours of 2 September, while Thomas Farynor, a baker, and his family slept above their shop in Pudding Lane, a spark from the oven downstairs started a fire. By the time it was discovered, the family was trapped. They escaped by climbing out of a window and across to the next house; but a maid who was too frightened to climb out died in the fire.

The fire spread quickly through the timber-framed buildings. At first, people weren't worried, because fires were common. Each district was supposed to keep buckets, ladders, axes and hooks for putting fires out. Pudding Lane wasn't far from the River Thames, so there was a plentiful supply of water. However, most people busied themselves with escaping from the fire instead of fighting it. The primitive fire engines used at that time proved to be useless. Meanwhile, strong winds whipped up the flames, which quickly spread from house to house. The buildings were tinder-dry after months of drought, so they caught fire easily. On 4 September, St Paul's Cathedral was engulfed by the flames. Samuel Pepys recorded in his diary: 'The churches, houses, and all on fire and flaming at once; and a horrid noise the flames made, and the cracking of houses at their ruins.' King Charles ordered buildings to be pulled down to try to stop the fire from reaching the Tower of London, where a large supply of gunpowder was stored. The fire finally burned itself out on 6 September.

fire facts

The Great Fire of London:

- destroyed 436 acres (176 hectares) of London

- burned down 13,200 houses and 87 churches

- finally brought the Great Plague to an end, because it killed the rats carrying the fleas that spread the disease.

Samuel Pepys surveys the Great Fire of London

Rebuilding London

Within a few days, the King started receiving plans for rebuilding London. All sorts of people had suggestions for how England's capital city should be rebuilt. Christopher Wren wanted to build a new city with a new layout and wide avenues, but the King feared it would take too long and be too expensive. It was decided to follow the existing layout, although some of the medieval streets were straightened and widened to make it harder for another fire to jump across them. The new buildings were built from brick or stone instead of wood, and had to comply with strict new building regulations. Six commissioners were put in charge of the rebuilding; Wren was one of them. He oversaw the rebuilding of more than 50 churches, but his prize project was St Paul's Cathedral. He had wanted to rebuild the cathedral even before the fire. Now he had the chance to start from scratch with a new building of his own design.

His first three designs for a new St Paul's were rejected. His fourth design finally

received approval. He cleverly got permission to make small changes to the design as he went along, without having to get consent every time. He took full advantage of this to change the cathedral from what had been approved into what he wanted to build. He gave the new St Paul's a great dome modelled on the dome of St Peter's Basilica in Rome. Rebuilding began in 1675 and was not completed until 1711. Some people loved Wren's cathedral, but others hated it. Whatever they thought of it, it quickly became one of London's most famous and instantly recognised buildings.

St Paul's: the old cathedral (left) and the new

Nell Gwynne

King Charles II's most famous mistress was Nell Gwynne. She was one of the first actresses in England; when the king reopened the theatres after the Puritan closures, he made it legal for women to appear on the stage.

At first, Nell sold oranges to theatre audiences. Then she joined a company of actors. She caught the King's eye while they were both watching a play, and became his mistress. Shortly before Charles died, he is reported to have said, 'Let not poor Nelly starve.' The new king settled her debts and paid her a pension.

Heir we go again!

Charles II had no children with his wife, Catherine of Braganza, and none of the children he had with his many mistresses were entitled to inherit the throne. When he died in 1685, his brother James became king. At first, King James II was popular, but it wasn't long before his beliefs started causing problems.

17th-century scientists

The 17th century was a time of great progress and advancement in science. The Royal Society was formed in 1660 to enable scientists to meet and discuss their discoveries.

William Harvey (1578–1657)
The first to give an accurate description of the circulation of blood around the human body.

Robert Hooke (1635–1703)
An architect, astronomer and scientist who invented several mechanical devices, including the universal joint, and wrote the first ever book on microscopy. He was also one of the six commissioners who oversaw the rebuilding of London after the Great Fire.

Sir Isaac Newton (1642–1727)
Thought by many to be the greatest scientist of his age, Newton formulated universal laws of gravitation and motion. He also studied the nature of light and invented an efficient reflecting telescope.

Edmond Halley (1656–1742)
The scientist, astronomer and mathematician after whom Halley's Comet is named, because he accurately calculated its orbit.

A Catholic king

James II

Royal house:	House of Stuart
Reigned:	1685–1688
Born:	14 October 1633
Place of birth:	St James's Palace, London
Father:	King Charles I
Mother:	Henrietta Maria of France
Died:	16 September 1701
Place of death:	Saint-Germain-en-Laye, France

James II was Catholic. Within a year of becoming king, he faced a rebellion led by the Protestant Duke of Monmouth, an illegitimate son of Charles II. Monmouth's army was defeated at the Battle of Sedgemoor on 6 July 1685. The rebels were dealt with in a series of trials called the Bloody Assizes, because the judges handed out such brutal punishments. Three hundred rebels were executed. Monmouth's execution was botched: it took several blows of the axe to remove his head.

James made himself even more unpopular by appointing Catholics to senior positions and trying to abolish anti-Catholic laws. He dismissed or prosecuted anyone who disagreed with him. He also increased the size of his army, to make it more difficult for anyone to dislodge him from the throne. Parliament objected to James's behaviour, so he dissolved it. By now, most of James's subjects wanted rid of him. His opponents hoped he would die soon and be replaced by Princess Mary, his Protestant daughter from his first marriage. When James and his second wife, Mary of Modena, had a son in 1688, ensuring a Catholic succession, there was panic and anger throughout the country.

The 'Glorious Revolution'

A group of Protestant noblemen invited William of Orange, the Dutch head of state and Princess Mary's husband, to invade England and take the throne. When William arrived in England on 5 November 1688, the English army and navy deserted James and supported William. James fled to France. William and Mary were now appointed joint monarchs. This change in the monarchy without bloodshed became known as the

'Glorious Revolution'. Parliament made William and Mary agree to obey the law and not to raise money without Parliament's permission. They were also not allowed to have their own army. These conditions were set out in a Bill of Rights, which also barred Catholics from being king or queen of England, and even barred English monarchs from marrying a Catholic. (These provisions are still in force today.)

In France, James plotted his return to England. In March 1689, he landed in Ireland, where he was still popular, with 6,000 French soldiers. William sent an army to Ireland, but it made little progress; he grew impatient and in June 1690 he went to Ireland himself to take control. He met James's army at the River Boyne, near Drogheda. On 1 July 1690, William's troops crossed the river and attacked James's army. There was no clear winner of the Battle of the Boyne, but James's failure to triumph persuaded him that he stood little chance of victory in Ireland and no chance at all in England. He left for exile again in France and never returned, though some of his supporters fought on for a while.

Joint monarchs

William III

Royal house: House of Orange
Reigned: 1689–1702
Born: 4 November 1650
Place of birth: Binnenhof, The Hague
Father: William II, Prince of Orange
Mother: Mary Henrietta, Princess Royal
(daughter of King Charles I)
Died: 8 March 1702
Place of death: Kensington Palace, London

Mary II

Royal house: House of Stuart
Reigned: 1689–1694
Born: 30 April 1662
Place of birth: St James's Palace, London
Father: King James II and VII
Mother: Lady Anne Hyde
Died: 28 December 1694
Place of death: Kensington Palace, London

Glencoe

After his victory in Ireland, William turned his attention to Scotland, where there was still some support for James. He demanded that the clans (Scottish family groups) swear allegiance to him, and he gave them a deadline: 1 January 1692. Some members of the MacDonald clan were late in taking the oath, possibly through no fault of their own. The Secretary of State in Edinburgh, John Dalrymple, was a Lowland Scotsman and Protestant who wanted Scotland to unite with England and disliked the Highland clans. He seized the opportunity to take action against the MacDonalds. He chose a rival clan, the Campbells, to do his dirty work.

When 120 soldiers under the command of Captain Robert Campbell arrived in Glencoe – supposedly to collect taxes – the MacDonalds gave them accommodation. However, on the morning of 13 February 1692, while a blizzard blew outside, the soldiers were ordered to kill the Campbells. Some refused to carry out their orders and were arrested. Thirty-eight MacDonalds were killed; dozens more died later in the freezing temperatures outdoors after their homes had been burned down. This terrible event is remembered as the Glencoe Massacre. An inquiry found that the killings were murder, but no-one stood trial. Dalrymple resigned.

Smallpox

Queen Mary enjoyed good health for most of her life, but in 1694 she caught smallpox. The disease was widespread in Europe at this time, causing hundreds of thousands of deaths every year. Mary died on 28 December. William had relied heavily on her. He was away for long periods with his troops, fighting against the French during the Nine Years' War; while he was away, Mary had ruled alone. The war ended in 1697 with the French king, Louis XIV, recognising William as the rightful king of England and agreeing not to support James II's claim to the throne any more. This removed a serious threat to William's rule.

As William grew older, the same old question came up: who was to succeed him? He had no children. Mary's sister Anne could inherit the throne herself but, as none of her 17 children had survived to adulthood, her death would end the Stuart line. To stop James II's Catholic descendants from returning, Parliament 'fixed' the succession. It passed an act that allowed a distant German relative of Anne's, Princess Sophia of Hanover, to succeed Anne.

In 1702, William suffered a fall from his horse and broke his collarbone. He developed pneumonia and died on 8 March. His horse had stumbled on a mole-hole. James II's supporters, known as Jacobites, gleefully toasted the mole as 'the little gentleman in the black velvet waistcoat'.

And so James's daughter Anne became queen. She was not a well woman. She couldn't walk at her coronation because of gout, and had to be carried in a sedan chair. Almost immediately, England was at war again. This time, it was the War of the Spanish Succession, which successfully prevented a union between two of England's most powerful enemies, France and Spain.

The last of the Stuarts

Queen Anne

Royal house: House of Stuart
Reigned: 1702–1714
Born: 6 February 1665
Place of birth: St James's Palace, London
Father: King James II
Mother: Lady Anne Hyde
Died: 1 August 1714
Place of death: Kensington Palace, London

Queen Anne's Revenge

There was a great upsurge in piracy at sea during Queen Anne's reign. It is sometimes called the Golden Age of Piracy. Blackbeard (Edward Teach), the most notorious of all pirates, lived at this time. He called his ship *Queen Anne's Revenge.*

Great Britain

In 1707, Parliament moved to bring the unruly Scots under control, so that they couldn't impose a Catholic monarch against the wishes of the English. It successfully pressured the Scots to accept an Act of Union that united Scotland and England under the same Parliament and monarch. The nation was now called the United Kingdom of Great Britain. (Wales had already been annexed to England in the time of Henry VIII.)

Queen Anne fell ill at the beginning of 1713. She suffered several bouts of illness over the next year and died on 1 August 1714. Her body was so swollen with infection that she was buried in an almost square coffin. Her designated heir, Princess Sophia of Hanover, had died a few weeks earlier, so the British crown now passed to Sophia's son George, the first of a new royal house – the House of Hanover.

How they lived and died in Stuart times

Life under the Stuarts was no easier for ordinary people than it had been in the Tudor age before it.

- **Population:** About 5 million people lived in England by the end of the Stuart period in the early 1700s. London's population more than doubled, from about 200,000 in 1600 to 500,000 in 1700. Other towns and cities were growing too, but most people still lived and worked on the land.

- **Work:** Ordinary people worked long hours. The average working week in the early 1700s was about 80 hours, or double the length of the working week today. And there were no holidays!

- **Disease:** When the Great Plague swept through England in 1665, it killed about a third of the population. Smallpox was widespread too, and measles was a killer disease. Water was likely to be infected with waterborne diseases like cholera, so beer and wine were drunk instead.

- **Life expectancy:** People didn't live much longer in the 17th century than they had in the previous century. Average life expectancy was about 36 years in 1700.

King George III
in his coronation robes

CHAPTER FOUR

THE HOUSE OF HANOVER

With the House of Hanover*
in power, Britain and
Ireland now had a German
king, George I. Hanoverian
monarchs would rule
Britain in an unbroken line for the next 187
years. Their rule would see a vast expansion
of the British Empire around the globe,
but also the loss of British colonies in
North America.

---

* Hanover *is the traditional spelling used by British historians;
in modern German the name is spelt* Hannover.

Your handy guide to the Hanoverian kings and queens of Britain and Ireland

Monarch	Reigned
George I	1714–1727
George II	1727–1760
George III	1760–1820
George IV	1820–1830
William IV	1830–1837
Victoria	1837–1901

Handel and George I

George Frideric Handel (or Georg Friedrich Händel; 1685–1759) was the leading composer in Georgian England. When the German-born composer visited England in 1710, he was already an employee of Prince George, the Elector of Hanover. His work was greeted enthusiastically in England and he decided to stay on – without his employer's permission. Fortunately, when George became king of England, he seems to have forgiven this slight.

Handel's most famous works are the oratorio (religious composition for solo voices, chorus and orchestra) *The Messiah,* and an orchestral suite composed for George I, the *Water Music.*

George I

George I spoke little English, so he left the business of government to a council of ministers. He had married his cousin Sophia in 1682, but the marriage failed; George preferred the company of his mistress. When Sophia had an affair, her lover was murdered and her marriage to George dissolved, but she wasn't allowed to leave and make a new life. George had her locked away in a castle in Lower Saxony for the rest of her days.

Revolting Jacobites

Many people were unhappy with George's selection as king. Some thought James Stuart, the son of King James II, should have inherited the throne. In 1715, a Jacobite rebellion to put James on the throne began in Scotland. At first, the rebels were successful. In December, James Stuart arrived in Scotland. However, in the face of Hanoverian forces swelled by Dutch reinforcements, the rebellion collapsed and James Stuart fled back into exile.

first of the Hanoverians
George I

Royal house: House of Hanover
Reigned: 1714–1727
Born: 28 May 1660
Place of birth: Hanover, Lower Saxony, Germany
Father: Ernest Augustus, Elector of Hanover
Mother: Countess Palatine Sophia of Simmen
Died: 11 June 1727
Place of death: Schloss Osnabrück, Lower Saxony

The first English political parties, the Whigs and the Tories, had formed during the reign of Charles II. When George learned that some Tories supported his enemies, the Jacobites, he chose the Whigs to form a government. They removed Tories from senior positions and dominated Parliament for decades, a period called the Whig Supremacy.

The bubble bursts!

The government nearly fell in 1720 because of the extraordinary event known as the South Sea Bubble. The South Sea Company, which had the sole right to trade with South America, had been set up in 1711 to raise money for the government. Individuals could invest by buying shares in the company. In return, the share owners received part of the company's profits. The investment, backed by the government, seemed to be a sure-fire winner. The demand for shares rose and so did their value. However, the South Sea Company failed to make the expected profits. When war with Spain broke out in 1718, the Spanish seized the company's offices and property in South America. Even so, it carried on selling shares for higher and higher prices.

In 1720 the share price suddenly crashed, like a bubble bursting. The shares were worthless. One of the thousands who lost money was the great scientist Sir Isaac Newton. After an inquiry, the Chancellor of the Exchequer (the finance minister) and several senior politicians were expelled from Parliament.

The last foreign king

George I suffered a stroke and died during a visit to Hanover in 1727. His son, George II, was the last British monarch to be born outside Britain. George II had a poor relationship with his eldest son, Frederick, Prince of Wales, who became a focus for opposition to the King. Relations become so bad that George banished his own son and heir from court.

George was keen to go to war, but Parliament managed to keep Britain at peace until 1739, when the War of Jenkins' Ear broke out. The British ship *Rebecca* had been boarded by the Spanish in 1731 and searched for smuggled goods. The captain, Robert Jenkins, was tied to a mast and his left ear was sliced off with a sword. This, together with continuing poor relations with Spain, led to Britain declaring war on Spain in 1739. Britain was then drawn into the War of the Austrian Succession, and George finally had his chance to go to war. He led British troops to victory against the French at the Battle of Dettingen in 1743. This was the last time a British monarch led an army into battle.

George II

Royal house: House of Hanover
Reigned: 1727–1760
Born: 30 October 1683
Place of birth: Hanover
Father: King George I
Mother: Sophia Dorothea of Celle
Died: 25 October 1760
Place of death: Kensington Palace, London

Rule, Britannia!

The popular patriotic song 'Rule, Britannia!' started as a poem, written by James Thomson in 1740. It was set to music by the composer Thomas Arne, and formed the grand finale of a masque (later reworked as an opera) about King Alfred, the supposed founder of the Royal Navy. When it was performed in London in 1745, it quickly became popular.

When Britain first at Heav'n's command
Arose from out the azure main,
This was the charter of the land,
And guardian angels sung this strain:

Rule, Britannia, rule the waves!
Britons never will be slaves.

Jacobites revolt... again!

The Jacobites made one final attempt to seize the throne in 1745. This time, their leader was Charles Edward Stuart, also known as the Young Pretender or Bonnie Prince Charlie. He was the grandson of the deposed Stuart king, James II.

With thousands of British soldiers away fighting in Europe, Charles decided that the time was right for rebellion. He made a perilous voyage from France to Scotland, narrowly avoiding being sunk by a British warship. With support from the Highland clans, Charles marched on Edinburgh and took the city. The Jacobite forces went on to win the Battle of Prestonpans – then they decided to march south and invade England.

They took Carlisle and Preston, and continued south. When news reached London that the Jacobites were coming, panic spread. However, the Jacobite leaders had already calculated that they could not defeat the armies they would likely meet on the way to London, and decided to return to Scotland. As they retreated in 1746, chased by government troops, they suffered a series of defeats.

Culloden

The final action of the rebellion was the Battle of Culloden. Jacobite and government armies met near Inverness on 16 April 1746. The Jacobites were defeated in less than an hour. Bonnie Prince Charlie fled to the Hebrides (a group of islands off the west coast of Scotland) and spent months hopping from island to island with government troops on his heels.

Bonnie Prince Charlie

Over the sea to Skye

While Bonnie Prince Charlie was hiding from government troops on the island of Benbecula, he met a local woman, Flora MacDonald. She helped him to escape by disguising him as her Irish maid, Betty Burke, on a boat trip to the Isle of Skye. He was picked up by a French warship and returned to France. Flora MacDonald was arrested and spent a year in the Tower of London, but was later released. The Jacobite challenge to the English throne was finally over.

The Skye Boat Song

Bonnie Prince Charlie's escape to the Isle of Skye is commemorated in a famous song written in the 1870s. The chorus goes:

Speed, bonnie boat, like a bird on the wing,
'Onward!' the sailors cry;
Carry the lad that's born to be king
Over the sea to Skye.

128

Crushing the clans

The government in London set out to crush the Scottish clans once and for all. Jacobite supporters were rounded up and imprisoned or executed. Their families were stripped of their estates. Laws were introduced to make it illegal for men, apart from soldiers in the British Army, to wear traditional tartan clothing or kilts. It was even illegal to play the bagpipes. Broadswords, the traditional Highland weapons, had to be given up to the authorities too. And government troops were stationed in the Highlands, so they could react quickly to put down any further rebellion.

God Save the King!

In the 1740s, the Jacobites and Royalists sang songs as a show of support for their leaders. One of these songs, 'God save the King', became the national anthem of Great Britain. It is still sung today (as 'God save the Queen'), although a verse in the original song about crushing the Scots is not usually included now! The music is sometimes attributed to the appropriately named Elizabethan composer John Bull.

10 Downing Street

The house known as 'Number 10' has been the home and workplace of the British prime minister since George II's reign.

- **Name:** The street is named after Sir George Downing, who built the houses in the 1680s for 'persons of good quality'. Downing had worked as a spy for Oliver Cromwell and for King Charles II.

- **Official residence:** George II acquired the house and presented it to Robert Walpole, the first British prime minister, in 1732. Walpole refused to accept it as a personal gift and so it became the official residence of the prime minister.

- **Enlargement:** It was enlarged by the architect William Kent, who connected it to two neighbouring houses to make the modern Number 10. The enlarged property has about 100 rooms.

- **Repairs:** The house has needed frequent repairs, because it was cheaply built with shallow foundations on soft ground.

- **Rebuilding:** It was in danger of collapsing altogether in the 1960s and most of it had to be rebuilt.

Britain in India

Envious of the overseas empires established by Spain and Portugal in the 15th and 16th centuries, Britain set about creating its own empire. It established colonies in the Americas, Africa, Asia and Australia. One of the most valuable parts of the Empire was India. In Victorian times, it would be described as 'the jewel in the crown'.

The British had been in India since 1600, when the East India Company was set up with royal approval to trade with the East Indies (the countries of south and southeast Asia). The Company expanded and even employed its own soldiers to protect its property, people and trade routes.

The French were in India too. During the Seven Years' War, the fighting in Europe spread to French and British forces elsewhere in the world, including India. When the East India Company strengthened its defences in Calcutta, they angered the local ruler, the Nawab of Bengal, leading to the infamous incident of the 'Black Hole of Calcutta'.

The Black Hole of Calcutta

In June 1756, the Nawab of Bengal ordered the British to stop work on Fort William, their base in Calcutta. When they ignored him, the Nawab's army surrounded the fort. Most of the British troops escaped, leaving a small contingent behind. When the fort fell, 146 men were captured and locked in the fort's jail, a small room known as the 'black hole'. In the airless heat and cramped conditions, with no food or drink, most of the men died within hours. When the room was opened the next day, only 23 were still alive. The story had a powerful effect in Britain, although historians now think the numbers may have been exaggerated.

When details of the British deaths in the Black Hole of Calcutta reached England, a British officer called Robert Clive was sent to India to take reprisals. East India Company troops led by Clive defeated French and Indian forces at the Battle of Plassey in 1757. The East India Company controlled most of the subcontinent until 1784, when the Company was brought under British government control.

Sport and games

The Georgians enjoyed playing sports and games, and watching them. Cricket, boxing and horse-racing became popular at this time. Boxing matches in Georgian England were bare-knuckle fights with no rules. The first English boxing champion was James Figg, in 1719. The bouts were so brutal that boxers sometimes died in the ring. The first rules to protect boxers, along with padded gloves, were not introduced until the 1740s.

The British Museum

In 1753 the eminent physician Sir Hans Sloane, who had attended Queen Anne, George I and George II, died. Sloane had been a collector of oddities and curiosities all his life. When he died, he left his collection of books, coins, drawings, plants, animals and all sorts of other things to the nation. Together with George II's royal library, it was put on display to the public in 1759 in London to form the British Museum. It grew and grew, becoming one of the world's greatest museums.

Dr Johnson and his dictionary

The printed word was more widely available in the 18th century than ever before. There were books, newspapers, essays, and political and religious pamphlets. But the rules of spelling and grammar were much more fluid than they are now. In 1746, a group of booksellers in London hired the author Samuel Johnson to compile a dictionary to put this right.

Johnson was known for his irritability and impatience. He also suffered from strange tics and depression that he feared were signs of insanity. But he worked tirelessly on his dictionary. It took him nine years. His work was detailed and meticulous, and far from boring. The text is peppered with Johnson's wit and opinions, including:

- **Excise:** 'a hateful tax'.

- **Oats:** 'A grain which in England is generally given to horses, but in Scotland supports the people'.

Johnson's *Dictionary of the English Language* was a massive book, published in two volumes in 1755, with 2,300 pages and more than 42,000 entries. It set the standard for all the dictionaries that followed.

Annus Mirabilis

Britain was at war with France again in 1756. At first, the war (called the Seven Years' War, for obvious reasons) went badly for Britain. But in 1759, everything went right – it was such a good year that it was called the *Annus Mirabilis* (Latin for 'wonderful year').

British forces won victories against the French in India, the West Indies and Prussia (Germany). A planned French invasion of Britain was thwarted too. The Royal Navy proved itself to be the world's most powerful naval force. The year ended with news that British troops under the command of General Wolfe had defeated the French in Canada, though Wolfe himself was killed during the Battle of Quebec. This and other victories ended French control of North America.

Britain was now the world's dominant colonial power, with the world's most powerful navy. Another run of victories against France and Spain three years later led to 1762 being called the Second Annus Mirabilis.

Time at sea

Long-distance sea voyages were risky in the 1700s, because navigation methods were so basic. Sailors could find out their latitude – how far north or south of the Equator they were – by measuring the height of the sun, or a known star, above the horizon. But they had no way to find out their longitude – how far east or west they had travelled. For this, they needed a clock that would keep good time on a rolling, pitching ship for weeks or months.

In 1714, a government commission offered a cash prize to anyone who could find a way to measure longitude accurately. In 1730, a clockmaker called John Harrison came up with a promising design, which he called H1. It took him five years to build it. In 1736 he tested it successfully on a voyage to Lisbon, Portugal, and back. He went on to design an even better clock, the H2. This couldn't be tested at sea, because Britain was at war and the precious clock couldn't be allowed to fall into enemy hands. By the time he made his next clock, the H3, other clockmakers were producing watches that kept time as well as

Harrison's large clocks. So he made his next timepiece, the H4, in the shape of a large pocket-watch. It lost only five seconds on a transatlantic voyage.

Harrison applied for the £20,000 prize for producing such an accurate marine clock, but he was refused. He gave his next watch, H5, to King George III to test. With the King's help, he was paid, but received less than half of the money promised. He died three years later, in 1776.

Punishing criminals

Crime was widespread in Georgian England.

- **Highway robbery:** Highwaymen like Dick Turpin preyed on travellers.
- **Picking pockets:** Pickpockets and cutpurses stole from people on the streets.
- **Burglary:** House-breakers stole from homes.
- **Poor:** The poor stole food because they were hungry, though they risked severe punishment.

About 200 crimes, including stealing food, were punishable by hanging. Huge crowds gathered to see criminals being executed.

Georgian art and design

Art, literature, music and architectural design flourished in Georgian Britain. During the 18th century, England saw the rise of the middle class, a group of people who were not aristocrats or landowners, but were literate and wealthy enough to have time for reading, listening to music and attending the theatre, ballet and opera. They wanted to be seen in the right places, wearing the most fashionable clothes. They also lavished a great deal of time and effort on furnishing and decorating their homes. They created a growing demand for the work of writers, composers, artists, architects, furniture makers and designers.

One of the foremost architects of the 18th century was Robert Adam, a Scot. In the 1750s, he went on a Grand Tour of Europe and learned from leading artists and architects of the day, including the famous Italian engraver of architectural scenes, Piranesi. When Adam returned to Britain, he set up his own business in London, designing grand public buildings, churches, mausoleums and private houses.

Georgian writers and artists

Daniel Defoe (c.1661–1731)
Journalist and author of *Robinson Crusoe*.

William Hogarth (1697–1764)
Versatile painter and engraver who satirised public life and private morality.

Henry Fielding (1707–1754)
Playwright and author of novels including *The History of Tom Jones, a Foundling*.

Sir Joshua Reynolds (1723–1792)
Artist who painted portraits in a grand style. Liked by George III, who knighted him.

Thomas Gainsborough (1727–1788)
Studied under Hogarth, known for portraits and landscapes.

William Wordsworth (1770–1850)
Romantic poet, author of 'Daffodils'.

Samuel Taylor Coleridge (1772–1834)
Poet known for *The Rime of the Ancient Mariner* and the unfinished *Kubla Khan*.

Jane Austen (1775–1817)
Novelist, best known for *Pride and Prejudice*.

J. M. W. Turner (1775–1851)
Landscape painter in a daringly abstract style.

John Constable (1776–1837)
Quintessential painter of English landscapes.

Mary Shelley (1797–1851)
Wrote the Gothic horror novel *Frankenstein*.

Prime ministers

Monarchs had been more dependent on Parliament since their powers were limited after the Glorious Revolution. In the Georgian period, power shifted even more from the monarch to Parliament. The process started with George I, who didn't speak English and was more interested in his German kingdoms, and so relied heavily on his ministers. The power of Parliament continued to grow as the power of the monarch declined.

- In Georgian times, 'prime minister' was a term of abuse. It described someone who acted above his position, because the monarch was thought to be the prime (first) minister.

- The first prime minister, although he refused the title, was Sir Robert Walpole, a member of the Whig Party. He served as prime minister from 1721 to 1742, during the reigns of George I and II. He was happier to be called 'First Lord of the Treasury', a post still held by the prime minister today.

- The term 'prime minister' was not used in official documents until 1905.

Birth of a movement

During the 18th century, a new religious movement called Methodism was born and spread throughout the country. A rector's son called John Wesley and some of his fellow students at Oxford University, members of a group called the Holy Club, believed in living a holy life, studying the Bible and helping the poor.

Wesley had worked as a minister in America, where he was influenced by the Moravian Church, a Protestant movement which had begun in eastern Europe. When he returned to England, Wesley's unconventional beliefs meant that he was often barred from preaching in churches. He began holding outdoor services to reach people who did not attend traditional church services, especially in poor neighbourhoods. Some of his services attracted thousands of people. He is said to have travelled 250,000 miles (400,000 km) around Britain and Ireland, and held 40,000 services. By the time of Wesley's death in 1791, the Methodist movement he created had more than 70,000 members.

A new George

George II died suddenly and unexpectedly in 1760. Soon after rising on the morning of 25 October, he went to the toilet. His valet heard a crash and rushed in to find the king on the floor. He was lifted onto his bed, but died almost immediately. His son and heir, Prince Frederick, had died in 1751, so he was succeeded by his grandson, another George.

Unlike the first two Georges, George III was born in England and spoke English as his first language. He came to the throne as a young man of only 22. He was crowned alongside his wife, Princess Charlotte of Mecklenburg-Strelitz, whom he had met for the first time a fortnight earlier, on the day of their marriage!

forever together

George II left instructions that the sides of his coffin and his wife's coffin should be removed so that their remains could mingle.

George III

Royal house:	House of Hanover
Reigned:	1760–1820
Born:	4 June 1738
Place of birth:	Norfolk House, London
Father:	Frederick, Prince of Wales
Mother:	Augusta of Saxe-Gotha
Died:	29 January 1820
Place of death:	Windsor Castle

It took George III only two years to upset Parliament. He appointed his old tutor, the Earl of Bute, as prime minister. Bute was widely seen as unqualified for the job as he had spent only three years in Parliament, and that was 20 years earlier. He was unpopular both inside and outside Parliament and lasted less than a year before resigning.

After the Earl of Bute, George appointed four prime ministers in the next five years before he found a man he felt he could trust: Lord Frederick North. North was fiercely loyal to George. However, he led Britain into a disastrous war with America.

Cook's travels

James Cook was one of the most famous explorers of the Georgian period. He was born in 1728 in a small village in Yorkshire. At the age of 17, he moved to Whitby on the coast and worked for a coal merchant. He must have seen ships coming and going all the time. In 1755, he joined the Royal Navy and went to sea himself. While serving in North America, he learned how to survey and chart coastal waters – and he proved to be very good at it.

In 1768 he was chosen to captain a ship called the *Endeavour* on an expedition the following year to the South Pacific to observe a rare transit of the planet Venus across the Sun. Secretly, he was also tasked to search for the southern continent that was thought to lurk at the bottom of the world.

He sailed to New Zealand and mapped the whole coast. Then he continued west, becoming the first European to see the east coast of Australia. *Endeavour* ran aground on the Great Barrier Reef and had to be repaired before he could return to England. In 1772 he commanded HMS *Resolution* on another voyage to search for the southern continent. He got close to Antarctica, but had to turn back because of the extreme cold.

Cook navigated with the help of a very accurate marine chronometer called the K1. It was a copy of John Harrison's famous H4, the first pocket-watch capable of keeping accurate time at sea (see pages 136–137).

In 1776, Cook made another voyage in the *Resolution*, this time to search for the Northwest Passage that was thought to link the Atlantic and Pacific oceans north of America. Unable to find it, he sailed south to the Sandwich Islands (Hawaii today), which he had discovered on his outward voyage.

While he was there, one of his ship's boats was stolen by the islanders. On 14 February 1779, in an attempt to get the boat back, he tried to take a local chief hostage, but the islanders fought back and proved too much for *Resolution*'s crew. While Cook and his men were retreating, chased by the islanders, Cook was stabbed and died.

Losing America

By the 1760s, Britain's American colonies were becoming increasingly unhappy at the taxes they had to pay to Britain, especially as they had no members of parliament in Britain to represent them. A popular slogan in America at the time was, 'No taxation without represenation!' As unrest spread, Britain sent troops to impose law and order – and increased the taxes. The colonists decided that they no longer wished to be governed by Britain. Representatives of the 13 British colonies signed a Declaration of Independence on 4 July 1776.

The colonists formed a Continental Army under the command of George Washington: Britain and America were at war. The British had the upper hand to begin with. However, as Washington's army grew in strength and experience it began to get the better of the British. In September 1777 the British captured the American capital, Philadelphia, but an attempted invasion by British forces from Canada ended in defeat at Saratoga.

The changing battlefield

By the 18th century, the mounted knights and archers of previous centuries had gone for good. English soldiers in bright red tunics, earning them the nickname 'redcoats', were armed with muskets and artillery pieces. Horses were still used in large numbers on the battlefield but, instead of knights, they carried dragoons: fast, lightly armoured troops brandishing muskets and a type of slashing sword called a sabre.

The fighting *Turtle*

In 1776 the Americans used a submarine to attack British ships. It was the first use of a submarine in warfare. The egg-shaped craft, called the *Turtle*, was built in 1775 by David Bushnell. On the night of 6 September 1776, Sergeant Ezra Lee piloted the *Turtle* towards the British warship HMS *Eagle* in New York harbour. However, he failed to attach an explosive charge to the ship; the mine drifted away and exploded in the East River. The attack didn't fail altogether, because the British were forced to move their fleet to a safer anchorage.

The colonists' success at Saratoga encouraged Britain's old enemies – France, Spain and the Dutch – to support the rebels. The turning point came in 1781 when General Cornwallis was forced to surrender at Yorktown. It was the beginning of the end: the British realised they couldn't win. The war ended with the Treaty of Paris in 1783. America was an independent country.

The Boston Tea Party

One of the most famous events of the American War of Independence was the Boston Tea Party.

When ships laden with tea taxed by Britain arrived in Boston in 1773, enraged colonists threw the tea overboard. Tea taxes had actually been cut, but it made no difference: the colonists were protesting against having to pay tax to a government in which they had no representation.

fathers and sons in No. 10

A father and son have been prime minister twice in British history, both times during the reign of George III. And three of the four prime ministers were called William.

Forty-three years after George Grenville became prime minister in 1763, his son William became PM. In 1766, a more famous PM took office: William Pitt. His son, also called William, was PM twice, beginning in 1783. Pitt the Younger was the youngest ever British prime minister: he came to office at the age of only 24.

A new continent

Soon after Britain had lost America, it started developing another colony on the other side of the world. When Captain Cook returned from his voyage to Australia, he reported to the government that the new land was suitable for settlement. When Britain lost America, it also lost a place to send criminals to. To deal with overcrowding in prisons, the government now decided to start sending convicted criminals to Australia.

In 1788, the First Fleet of British settlers arrived in Australia. There were eleven ships. On board six of them were about 750 convicts – mostly men, but there were women and children too. The other ships carried stores, supplies, and marines to guard the convicts. Some of the marines brought their families with them. More than 20 convicts died during the passage – fewer than would die in later voyages. In January 1788, after eight months at sea, the ships landed at Botany Bay on Australia's east coast. The site proved to be unsuitable, so the settlers moved north to Port Jackson, New South Wales. There they established a penal colony under the governorship of Arthur Phillip.

The settlers had to support themselves, but the land was poor and they knew little about farming. Food had to be rationed. The settlers eventually found more fertile land where they could farm more successfully. The colony succeeded and grew. More colonies were established in other parts of Australia and

Tasmania. Over the next 65 years, the British would transport more than 162,000 convicts to Australia in 806 ships.

Science in the 1700s

The pace of scientific discovery quickened during the 1700s. The century became known as the Age of Enlightenment. It was a time when scientists tried to understand the natural world through reason and science instead of accepting old explanations that were often based on myths and legends. Chemists discovered new elements and compounds. Naturalists travelled the world finding new plants and animals. Physicians discovered new cures for old diseases.

Giants of 17th-century science such as Sir Isaac Newton and Edmund Halley were still doing important work, but now they were joined by a new generation of scientists.

The Age of Enlightenment laid the foundations of the Industrial Revolution, when engineers applied scientific discoveries to make new machines and structures.

18th-century scientists

Joseph Black (1728–1799)
French-born chemist who discovered carbon dioxide.

Henry Cavendish (1731–1810)
French-born chemist and physicist who discovered hydrogen, which he called 'inflammable air'.

Joseph Priestley (1733–1804)
English chemist who discovered oxygen, which he called 'dephlogisticated air'. He also invented soda water by dissolving carbon dioxide in water, and was the first person to make nitrous oxide (laughing gas).

William Herschel (1728–1822)
German-born astronomer who discovered the planet Uranus and two of its moons.

Joseph Banks (1743–1820)
English naturalist who accompanied James Cook to the South Pacific. He introduced eucalyptus, acacia, mimosa and banksia (which was named after him) to the western world.

Daniel Rutherford (1749–1819)
Scottish physician, chemist and botanist; the first person to isolate nitrogen from air.

Edward Jenner (1749–1823)
English physician and scientist who pioneered smallpox vaccination.

How the other half lived

How *life* changed in the 18th century
~ and how, for some, it didn't

In 18th-century Georgian England, power still rested with the aristocracy. Most people were poor and badly educated.

- **Population:** England's population grew rapidly in the second half of the 18th century. By 1800 it had reached about 8.5 million. London's population doubled, reaching a million by 1800. Towns in the Midlands and the north of England were growing quickly, too. Liverpool, Birmingham and Manchester all had populations of more than 70,000.

- **Women:** Women's lives had changed little for centuries. Women had no power or independence. They were totally under the control of the men in their lives – first their fathers and then their husbands. During the 18th century it was still very important for a woman to find a husband.

- **Education:** About two-thirds of children went to school by 1800. Working-class children only had about three years' schooling, because they had to work and earn money for the family from an early age.

- **Life expectancy:** Between 1700 and 1800, life expectancy in England increased from 36 to about 40.

The rise of the industrialist

CHAPTER FIVE

FROM FARM TO FACTORY

In the second half of the 18th century, England underwent revolutions in agriculture and industry. The population was growing faster than ever and the people had to be fed. Traditional farming methods were not up to the job, so improvements were essential. Meanwhile, in the towns and cities, new manufacturing methods using machines were transforming industry. These changes had far-reaching effects throughout English society.

Leaving the land

Following the Dissolution of the Monasteries by King Henry VIII, large tracts of land that had been owned by the monasteries were sold to raise money. The new landowners employed tenants to farm the land for them. Crops were grown on long, thin strips of land and animals were grazed on common land, but farming like this was inefficient. Since Tudor times, some landowners had combined the traditional strip fields to make larger fields that were more productive and therefore more profitable. These 'enclosures' gathered pace in the 18th century. New farming methods boosted productivity and profits even more.

The landowners employed only as many people as they needed, and only at the times of the year when they were needed the most – mainly for ploughing and harvesting. As a result, people whose families had farmed for generations found themselves without work. Many of them moved to the cities to look for jobs. There, they provided labour for the factories that were transforming England into the first industrial nation on Earth.

Turnip Townshend

If the same crop is grown on the same land year after year, nutrients in the soil are used up and pests and diseases thrive. The answer is crop rotation – dividing the land up into fields, growing different crops on each field and moving the crops from field to field every year. The traditional English system used three fields and left one field empty, or 'fallow', each year to rest between crops.

Viscount Charles Townshend (1674–1738) introduced a new crop rotation system from Holland. It used four fields and grew crops on all of them. Two main crops, such as wheat and barley, were grown on two of the fields. Clover was grown on the third field for grazing animals; it also fixed nitrogen from the air, making the soil more fertile. Turnips were grown on the fourth field, for animal feed. Each year, the four crops were rotated around the four fields. The four-field system made it possible to breed and feed more animals, and their manure enriched the soil. Townshend became known as 'Turnip' Townshend, from the use of turnips in his crop system.

Selective breeding

Farmers and landowners, including Robert Bakewell (1725–1795) and Thomas Coke (1754–1842), applied scientific methods to animal breeding. They started keeping the males and females apart, so that they could allow only the best animals to breed. Selective breeding, as this is called, doubled the weight of cattle and sheep during the 18th century.

farm machinery

Farmers started using more machines. In 1701, Jethro Tull (1674–1741) invented a machine called a seed drill. Seeds were normally sown by hand, with haphazard results: too much seed was sown in some places, not enough in other places. Tull solved this problem by building a machine that dug a channel in the ground, sowed the right amount of seed and then covered the seed with soil. He also invented a horse-drawn hoe to clear weeds between rows of plants, and improved the design of ploughs.

In 1730, Joseph Foljambe designed a new, lighter plough, called the Rotherham plough. This became the standard horse-drawn plough throughout England for the next 180 years, until the tractor replaced the horse.

In the 1780s, the mechanical engineer Andrew Meikle (1719–1811) invented a threshing machine to separate grain from the husks (outer seed coat) and stalks. Threshing had previously been very labour-intensive and time-consuming work. Harvested wheat was beaten with flails. Then it was 'winnowed' – thrown up in the air so that the lighter husks and stalks were blown away, leaving the grain behind. The first threshing machines were powered by horses, later ones by steam.

Shaping nature

The Agricultural Revolution made landowners very wealthy. Having improved on nature on their farms, they set about doing the same thing on their vast country estates. They employed a new type of artist, the landscape architect, to reshape the land around their homes with rolling lawns, lakes, woods and streams – all built by hand and positioned according to the landscape architect's plan. Some gardens had copies of classical Greek temples or specially built ruins to give them a fake history. This style of landcape design spread from England to Europe, where it was known as the *jardin anglais* (English garden).

Gardeners on a grand scale

- **William Kent** (1685–1748), one of the first English landscape architects, lived in Italy for 10 years and brought Italian ideas back to England with him. He designed the gardens at Chiswick House in London and Rousham House in Oxfordshire.

- **Charles Bridgeman** (1690–1738) redesigned the royal gardens at Windsor, Kensington Palace, Hampton Court, St James's Park and Hyde Park. He also designed the gardens at Stowe House in Buckinghamshire and several other grand houses.

- **Lancelot Brown** (1716–1783) is better known as 'Capability' Brown, because of his habit of telling landowners that their grounds had great capability for improvement. He designed more than 170 parks and gardens.

The Industrial Revolution

Agriculture wasn't the only industry to change dramatically during the 18th century. Manufacturing was changing too. Textile manufacture had been a cottage industry – the work was done by people working at home. Then a series of improvements to spinning and weaving machines enabled them to work faster and produce more cloth.

In weaving, thread has to be moved repeatedly from one side of the loom (weaving machine) to the other. This was done by hand until 1733, when John Kay (1704–c.1779) invented the flying shuttle. The shuttle, carrying the thread, was thrown by the machine from one side of the loom to the other. This enabled a loom to work faster, while being operated by one person instead of two. Another important invention was Arkwright's water frame, a water-powered spinning machine. Other industries experienced similar improvements, producing a revolution – the world's first Industrial Revolution.

Textile industry inventions

- **Flying shuttle** (1733): Invented by John Kay (1704–c.1779) to speed up cloth weaving.

- **Spinning jenny** (1764): Invented by James Hargreaves (1720–1778), it enabled a spinner to spin eight or more threads at once.

- **Water frame** (1769): A water-powered spinning machine invented by Richard Arkwright (1732–1792).

- **Spinning mule** (1779): A machine that could spin more than 1,000 threads at a time, invented by Samuel Crompton (1753–1827).

- **Power loom** (1784): The first powered loom was invented by Edmund Cartwright (1743–1823).

The changing face of work

The Industrial Revolution changed the way people worked. Instead of toiling on their own at home, workers had to go to the huge buildings where the new machines were. One of the first of these factories was built by Richard Arkwright, the inventor of the water frame. His five-storey cotton-spinning factory, called Cromford Mill, operated day and night with hundreds of workers, some as young as 7.

The steam age

Flooding was a constant problem in the deep tin mines of Devon and Cornwall. In 1698, Thomas Savery (c.1650–1715) invented a steam-powered siphon to take the water out, but it was not very effective. Then, in 1712, Thomas Newcomen (1664–1729) invented the machine that would change the world – the first practical steam engine. Newcomen's engines were in great demand, but when a Scottish engineer, James Watt (1736–1819), repaired a Newcomen engine, he found that it wasted a lot of energy. He designed his own steam engines that were more efficient. Watt formed a partnership with Matthew Boulton (1728–1809) to manufacture his engines.

At first, Boulton and Watt engines were used to pump water. Then Boulton suggested modifying the engines so that they could power all sorts of machines, not just pumps. This had a dramatic effect on manufacturing and the Industrial Revolution as a whole. Until then, mills and factories relied on water power and had to be built near rivers. Switching to steam power meant that they could be built anywhere. The pace of the revolution accelerated. It was also spreading to other countries, creating a growing demand for British steam engines, other machines and the products they made.

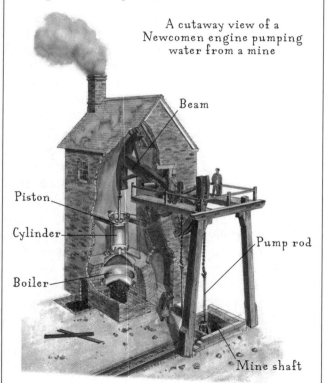

A cutaway view of a Newcomen engine pumping water from a mine

Beam

Piston

Cylinder

Pump rod

Boiler

Mine shaft

Making iron

The Industrial Revolution created a growing demand for iron. This was produced by burning charcoal, made from wood, to heat iron ore in a furnace. So much charcoal was needed that wood was in short supply. Then, in the early 1700s, Abraham Darby (1678–1717) found he could use coke, made from coal, instead of charcoal. Coal was plentiful, so he could make as much iron as his furnace could produce.

Coal mining

The need for fuel to make iron and to power the growing numbers of steam engines created an increasing demand for coal. By the early 1700s, most of the coal near the surface had been dug out, so miners had to go deeper and deeper underground in search of coal.

Despite the scientific and engineering advances above ground, very little machinery was used underground in mines. There was no room in the narrow tunnels and shafts for big, heavy machines, and steam engines would have poisoned the little fresh air that could be pumped below ground for the miners. So, the miners who worked to produce the coal that made the coke that produced the iron to make the machines for other industries worked without the help of machines themselves. Neverthelesss, between 1700 and 1800, coal production increased from 2.7 million to 10 million tonnes a year.

The first iron bridge

In the 18th century, business was booming around Coalbrookdale in Shropshire. However, the River Severn ran through the area and the only way to cross it was by boat. A bridge was needed. Until then, bridges had always been built from wood, stone or brick. Coalbrookdale was an iron-producing area, so this time the builders decided to construct their bridge from iron made in Abraham Darby's ironworks nearby. (This Abraham Darby was the grandson of the Abraham Darby who had started making iron at Coalbrookdale in the early 1700s.) The world's first iron bridge was completed in 1779 and it's still in use today.

How they toiled in mines and factories

Working conditions in the mines and factories of the Industrial Revolution were dirty and dangerous.

- **Hours:** It was common to have to work for 12 hours or more at a stretch.

- **Health and safety:** Factories were dusty, noisy, stuffy and hot. Workers who fell asleep or lost concentration could get caught up in the moving parts of machines.

- **Child labour:** Children were especially at risk, because their job was often to get into the narrow spaces between machines and underneath them to clear waste materials and blockages.

- **All in the family:** Whole families worked in mines. Fathers and sons hacked the coal out by hand. Mothers and children hauled it out of the mine. Accidents were common.

Lancashire mill workers

Transport

The Industrial Revolution needed good transport links. Raw materials and manufactured products had to be moved around the country. Supplies from other countries had to be moved from the ports to where they were needed. Finished products had to be transported to the ports to be shipped out to the rest of the world.

England's roads were in very poor condition in the 1700s – little better than dirt tracks in many places. It was easier to move goods and materials by boat. However, there wasn't always a convenient river available. The answer was to build artificial waterways – canals. Canals had been built in England since Roman times, but the Industrial Revolution spurred a golden age of canal building across the country, linking towns, cities, rivers and ports. The first major English transport canal, the Bridgewater Canal, opened in 1761.

One of the problems the canal builders faced was how to connect waterways that were at different heights, or levels. The answer was locks: narrow chambers fitted with watertight gates at each end. The boat was hauled into the chamber and the gates were closed behind it. Then water was allowed to flood into the lock, or drain out of it, to change the water level to match the next stretch of waterway. Finally, the gates at the other end were opened to let the boat continue on its way.

The next problem was how to propel the boats, or barges. Sails and oars were impractical in the narrow canals and there were no engines available yet, so the barges were pulled by horses walking on paths, called 'towpaths', alongside the canals. Tunnels were too narrow for the horses, so a different method, called 'legging', was used to propel the barges through tunnels. As a barge entered a tunnel, the crew lay on their backs and moved the barge along by pushing with their feet on the walls or roof of the tunnel.

18th-century English canals

These are a few of the dozens of canals built in England during the 18th century.

- **Bridgewater Canal:** Britain's first major canal, 39 miles (65 km) long, built to transport coal from the Duke of Bridgewater's mines at Worsley in Lancashire to Manchester. Opened in 1761.

- **Kennet and Avon Canal:** Two lengths of river and a canal linking Bristol and Reading. The river sections were made navigable in the 18th century. The canal opened in 1810. Length: 87 miles (140 km).

- **Trent and Mersey Canal:** Built between 1766 and 1777 to link the River Trent with the River Mersey; 93 miles (150 km) long.

- **Staffordshire and Worcestershire Canal:** Connects the River Severn to the Trent and Mersey Canal over a distance of 46 miles (74 km); opened in 1772.

- **Grantham Canal:** Opened in 1797 to transport coal from the River Trent to Grantham, Lincolnshire, a distance of 33 miles (53 km).

- **Oxford Canal:** Opened in 1774 to carry goods and materials between the Midlands and London. Length: 78 miles (126 km).

Master canal builder

One of the most important 18th-century canal builders was James Brindley (1716–1772). He showed a flair for engineering at a young age and was spotted by the Duke of Bridgewater. It was the Duke who got him involved in building canals.

Following his work on the Bridgewater Canal, his reputation spread and he was soon hired to build other canals. He had a grand plan to link the four great rivers of England (the Trent, Severn, Mersey and Thames) by canals. The Trent and Mersey Canal was to have been the first stage, but he wasn't able to complete his plan before he died. He built a total of 365 miles (587 km) of canals.

Who were the navvies?

Eighteenth-century canals were dug by workers using hand tools such as picks and spades. These hard-working diggers were known as 'navigators', or 'navvies', because they built navigation canals. Later, when railways began to replace canals as the nation's trade and transport arteries, the same term was used for those who worked on railway construction.

full steam ahead?

As soon as the steam engine was invented, engineers wondered if it could be used to power a vehicle. However, no really successful steam-powered land vehicles were built in the 18th century. The problem was that early steam engines worked at low pressure. Engineers hadn't yet learned how to build safe high-pressure boilers; when they tried, the engines had a habit of exploding! Low-pressure steam engines were enormous – far too big for a road carriage or railway locomotive. However, a small low-pressure engine was powerful enough to propel a boat.

Most of the early work on steamboats was done by Denis Papin and the Marquis Claude de Jouffroy in France and by John Fitch in America. Closer to home, Patrick Miller and William Symington built two steamboats in Scotland in the 1780s. Ten years later, Symington would start work on the boat that would make history as the first practical steamboat, the *Charlotte Dundas*. The first steamboat in England was not built until 1812.

Pay up!

To improve the poor state of roads in England, private companies called 'turnpike trusts' charged the public to use some roads. Some of the money raised was used to improve the roads; the rest was paid to those who invested in the companies. Gates at the ends of a road ensured that no-one could enter without paying. The spike-topped gates were called 'turnpikes'. By 1800, there were more than 700 turnpike trusts in Britain.

Road rage

Turnpike roads were unpopular with those who had been used to using roads free of charge. The gates that closed the turnpike roads to all but those who paid were often damaged or destroyed by angry road users. To discourage people from burning the gates or pulling them down, the destruction of turnpike gates was made a criminal offence punishable by execution.

What did the Industrial Revolution do for us?

The Industrial Revolution gave us:

- **The iron industry** to supply the iron needed to build machines and bridges.
- **The textile industry:** The production of cloth in large quantities in cotton mills.
- **Mass production:** Making products in large numbers using machines in factories.
- **Marketing and advertising** to sell products made in the new factories.
- **The canal network** to transport goods and materials, especially coal.
- **Better roads** to transport people, goods and materials.
- **Civil engineering** to build the bridges, aqueducts and tunnels needed for the canal network and improved roads.
- **The middle class:** a new section of society in addition to the poor, wealthy landowners and the aristocracy.
- **Steam engines** able to power a huge variety of machines.
- **Steamships** which freed shipping companies from reliance on the wind.
- **Railways** which made fast, long-distance land transport possible.

What happens next?

By the time this part of our story ends, around 1800, England has been transformed from a world of knights in armour, castles, longbowmen, all-powerful monarchs, public executions and illiterate peasants into a world of science, medicine, industry, stately homes, firearms, steam power, growing cities, a literate middle class and a parliament that holds more power than the monarch.

A century later, the steam age will be drawing to a close, railways will have spread across the country, and the first motorcars will be on the roads. Soon after this, the whole world will be plunged into wars more terrible than the English, or anyone else, have ever seen. These first modern wars will spur the development of new technology, including nuclear power, jet planes, radar and computers, that, along with radio and television, will transform England and the rest of the world.

This story continues in Volume 3.

A Tudor recipe

Felettes in Galentyne

Tudor recipes weren't like ours. A recipe was just a rough plan for making the dish. There were no quantities, temperatures or cooking times – cooks were supposed to work out all of that for themselves! This is a modern version of a recipe called *felettes in galentyne* (pork fillets in a meaty gravy), which appeared in a book printed in 1468.

Ingredients:
- 1 lb (450 g) pork (fore quarter)
- 2 medium onions
- 1 pint (600 ml) beef stock
- 1 teacup breadcrumbs
- 1 tsp vinegar
- salt, pepper, cinnamon, mace and one clove

Method:
1 Roast the pork until half cooked.
2 Chop the onions and fry them until brown.
3 Slice the roast pork into half-inch (1 cm) thick slices.
4 Put the pork and onions in a pot and add the stock.
5 Simmer for about an hour.
6 When nearly ready, thicken the gravy with the breadcrumbs and add the vinegar.
7 Season to taste with the salt and pepper.
8 For an authentic Tudor flavour, add the rest of the spices and serve while piping hot.

Royal reigns

Kings and queens of England

• **House of Wessex**
802–839 Egbert
839–858 Ethelwulf
858–860 Ethelbald
860–865 Ethelbert
865–871 Ethelred
871–899 Alfred the Great
899–924 Edward the Elder
924–939 Athelstan
939–946 Edmund
946–955 Eadred
955–959 Eadwig
959–975 Edgar
975–978 St Edward the
  Martyr
978–1013 Ethelred the
  Unready

• **House of Denmark**
1013–1014 Sweyn
  Forkbeard

• **House of Wessex**
1014–1016 Ethelred the
  Unready (again)
1016 Edmund Ironside

• **House of Denmark**
1016–1035 Canute (Cnut)
1035–1040 Harold
  Harefoot
1040–1042 Harthacnut

• **House of Wessex**
1042–1066 St Edward the
  Confessor
1066 Harold

• **House of Normandy**
1066–1087 William I,
  the Conqueror
1087–1100 William II
1100–1135 Henry I
1135–1154 Stephen
  (disputed with Matilda,
  in power 1141)

• **House of Plantagenet**
1154–1189 Henry II
1189–1199 Richard I,
  the Lionheart
1199–1216 John
1216–1272 Henry III
1272–1307 Edward I
1307–1327 Edward II
1327–1377 Edward III
1377–1399 Richard II

• **House of Lancaster**
1399–1413 Henry IV
1413–1422 Henry V
1422–1461 Henry VI

• **House of York**
1461–1470 Edward IV

- **House of Lancaster**
1470–1471 Henry VI
(again)

- **House of York**
1471–1483 Edward IV
(again)
1483 Edward V
1483–1485 Richard III

- **House of Tudor**
1485–1509 Henry VII
1509–1547 Henry VIII
1547–1553 Edward VI
1553 Jane Grey
(disputed)
1553–1558 Mary I
1558–1603 Elizabeth I

- **House of Stuart**
1603–1625 James I
of England and
VI of Scotland
1625–1649 Charles I

- **Commonwealth and
Protectorate**
1649–1660 no ruling
monarch

- **House of Stuart**
1660–1685 Charles II
1685–1688 James II
of England and
VII of Scotland
1689–1702 William III,
co-ruler with:
1689–1694 Mary II
1702–1707 Anne

Kings and queens of the United Kingdom

- **House of Stuart**
1707–1714 Anne

- **House of Hanover**
1714–1727 George I
1727–1760 George II
1760–1820 George III
1820–1830 George IV
1830–1837 William IV
1837–1901 Victoria

- **House of Wettin
(Saxe-Coburg-Gotha)**
1901–1910 Edward VII

- **House of Windsor**
1910–1936 George V
1936 Edward VIII
1936–1952 George VI
1952–present Elizabeth II

Glossary

abdicate To resign the position of king or queen.

annul To declare invalid. A marriage that is annulled is not simply ended – it never existed.

Archbishop of Canterbury The leader of the Church of England and, today, the head of the worldwide Anglican Church.

chivalry Courtesy, honour and gallantry – the noble qualities of a knight, or *chevalier*.

courtier A person in attendance at the court of a king or queen. Courtiers could be aristocrats, soldiers, clerks, secretaries or other trusted advisors.

cutpurse A thief who steals money by cutting the string attaching a purse to the victim's belt.

Dauphin The heir to the French throne. *Dauphin* means 'dolphin', because dolphins appear on the heir's coat of arms.

diplomat A person appointed by a monarch or government to represent a country abroad.

Divine Right of Kings The belief that a king's right to rule is God-given and so a king is not subject to any other authority, such as Parliament or the people.

interregnum The period between two royal reigns, when there is no acknowledged king or queen; in English history, the term usually refers to the Protectorate and Commonwealth period (1649–1660), between the reigns of Charles I and Charles II.

Jacobites Supporters of the deposed king, James II.

Lord Protector A prince or nobleman who ruled on behalf of a monarch who was too young to rule. Also, the head of state during the Interregnum (1649–1660) between the execution of King Charles I and the Restoration of the Monarchy.

microscopy The use of a microscope to study minute structures and organisms.

plague A deadly infectious disease caused by bacteria spread by the bites of infected fleas carried by rats.

pretender A person who claims a title or position he or she is not entitled to. Royal pretenders claimed the throne.

privateer A person or ship authorised by the government to attack the ships of enemy countries.

Puritans A group of English Protestants in the late 16th and 17th centuries who sought to rid the Church and state of all Catholic practices.

Reformation Events that led to some people in England and Europe rejecting Catholicism and forming their own Protestant churches, such as the Church of England.

Restoration of the Monarchy The return to royal government on the accession of Charles II in 1660.

sanctuary Until the 17th century, a church or other religious building where fugitives from the law could not be arrested.

sumptuary laws Laws that control or restrict people's consumption, especially the clothes, food and luxuries they can buy.

Tower of London A fortress by the River Thames in London, constructed in 1078 and extended later, used as a palace and prison. Today, it is a tourist attraction that houses the British crown jewels.

treason A crime committed against the monarch or state. Treason against the monarch is also called 'high treason'.

turnpike road A gated road that can be used only on payment of a toll.

A timeline of early modern England

1455 Wars of the Roses begin.

1483 The Duke of Gloucester seizes the throne as King Richard III.

1485 Richard III is killed at the Battle of Bosworth Field. Henry Tudor becomes King Henry VII.

1509 Henry VII dies and is succeeded by Henry VIII.

1536 Dissolution of the Monasteries begins.

1536 Henry VIII suffers a serious jousting accident.

1545 The warship *Mary Rose* sinks during a battle in the English Channel.

1547 Henry VIII dies and Edward VI becomes king.

1553 After Edward VI's death, Lady Jane Grey reigns for only nine days and is succeeded by Mary I.

1554 Mary I marries Prince Philip of Spain.

1558 Mary I dies and Elizabeth I becomes queen.

1561 The widowed Mary, Queen of Scots returns to Scotland from France.

1564 William Shakespeare is born in Stratford upon Avon.

1587 Mary, Queen of Scots is executed.

1588 The Spanish Armada makes an unsuccessful attempt to land an invading army in England; it is defeated by the English navy and by the weather.

1603 Elizabeth I dies and is succeeded by James VI of Scotland, who becomes James I, the first Stuart king of England.

1605 Guy Fawkes and other conspirators are arrested and executed for the Gunpowder Plot to kill James I.

1625 James I dies and is succeeded by his eldest surviving son, Charles I.

1629 Charles I dismisses Parliament.

1640 Charles I is forced to recall Parliament.

1642 Charles I enters Parliament and tries to arrest politicians who oppose him, which helps to provoke the English Civil War.

1642 The Battle of Edgehill, the first major battle of the Civil War, has no clear winner.

1644 The Battle of Marston Moor is won by the Parliamentarians.

1645 The New Model Army crushes the Royalists at the Battle of Naseby.

1647 Charles I falls into the hands of the Parliamentarians.

1648 The Battle of Preston, the final battle of the Civil War, is won by the Parliamentarians.

1649 Charles I is put on trial for treason, found guilty and executed. England is now ruled by Lord Protector Oliver Cromwell.

1651 Charles II is defeated at the Battle of Worcester and goes into exile on the Continent.

1658 Oliver Cromwell dies and is succeeded as Lord Protector by his son, Richard.

1659 Richard Cromwell resigns as Lord Protector.

1660 The monarchy is restored when Charles II returns to England and takes the throne.

1665 The Great Plague sweeps through London and some other areas.

1666 The Great Fire of London destroys most of the city.

1685 Charles II dies and is succeeded by James II.

1687 James II tries in vain to abolish anti-Catholic laws.

1688 James II and Mary of Modena have a son, a Catholic heir to the throne.

1688 The 'Glorious Revolution': William of Orange is invited by prominent English Protestants to invade

England from Holland. James II flees to France and William becomes king. His English wife becomes Queen Mary II.

1689 The Bill of Rights limits the power of the monarchy.

1689 James II lands in Ireland and begins a rebellion to reclaim the English throne.

1690 James is defeated by William at the Battle of the Boyne and returns to France.

1692 Members of the MacDonald clan are murdered at Glencoe by a rival clan, the Campbells, on the orders of the English government.

1694 Mary II dies from smallpox.

1702 William III dies and is succeeded by Queen Anne, the last Stuart monarch.

1707 The Act of Union unites England, Wales and Scotland, creating the United Kingdom.

1709 Abraham Darby discovers how to convert coal into coke and use it to produce iron.

c.1712 Thomas Newcomen invents his steam engine.

1714 Queen Anne dies and is succeeded by George I, the first Hanoverian monarch.

1715 The first Jacobite rebellion is a failure.

1720 The South Sea Bubble.

1721 Robert Walpole becomes the first prime minister.

1727 George I dies and is succeeded by George II.

1739 The War of Jenkins' Ear begins.

1743 George II leads his troops at the Battle of Dettingen, the last English monarch ever to do so.

1745 The second Jacobite rebellion begins.

1746 The second Jacobite rebellion ends in failure when the rebels lose the Battle of Culloden.

1756 British prisoners of the Nawab of Bengal die while imprisoned in a tiny room known as the Black Hole of Calcutta.

1757 East India Company troops under Colonel Robert Clive defeat the Nawab of Bengal at the Battle of Plassey.

1759 British forces under General James Wolfe defeat the French at the Battle of Quebec during the Seven Years' War.

1759 The British Museum opens to the public.

1760 George II dies and is succeeded by George III.

1761 The Bridgewater Canal, the first major transport canal in England, opens.

1770 Captain James Cook claims Australia for Britain.

1773 The Boston Tea Party: American colonists protest against paying British taxes.

1776 Britain's former American colonies sign the Declaration of Independence.

1779 The world's first iron bridge is built over the River Severn at Coalbrookdale, Shropshire.

1783 The Treaty of Paris ends the American War of Independence.

1788 The first British settlers arrive in Australia.

1788 George III suffers his first major bout of mental illness.

1791 William Wilberforce introduces his first anti-slavery bill in Parliament.

1797 Royal Navy sailors mutiny at Spithead, near Portsmouth, and Nore, in the Thames Estuary, demanding better pay and conditions.

1798 Admiral Nelson defeats the French fleet at the Battle of the Nile.

1798 An uprising in Ireland fails to overthrow British rule.

1799 Prime Minister William Pitt the Younger introduces income tax for the first time in Britain.

Index

The Cherished Library

Edited by Stephen Haynes

A CLASSIFIED LIST
OF THE FIRST 43 VOLUMES

Available in hardback binding
and for all digital platforms

Very Peculiar Histories™

History of the British Isles
England (in 3 volumes)
    Vol. 1: From Ancient Times to Agincourt
      David Arscott 978-1-908973-37-5
    Vol. 2: From the Wars of the Roses to the
      Industrial Revolution *Ian Graham* 978-1-908973-38-2
    Vol. 3: From Trafalgar to the New Elizabethans
      John Malam 978-1-908973-39-9
    Boxed set of all three volumes: 978-1-908973-41-2
Scotland (in 2 volumes) *Fiona Macdonald*
    Vol. 1: From Ancient Times to Robert the Bruce
      978-1-906370-91-6
    Vol. 2: From the Stewarts to Modern Scotland
      978-1-906714-79-6
Ireland *Jim Pipe* 978-1-905638-98-7
Wales *Rupert Matthews* 978-1-907184-19-2

History of the 20th century
Titanic *Jim Pipe* 978-1-907184-87-1
World War One *Jim Pipe* 978-1-908177-00-1
World War Two *Jim Pipe* 978-1-908177-97-1
The Blitz *David Arscott* 978-1-907184-18-5
Rations *David Arscott* 978-1-907184-25-3
The 60s *David Arscott* 978-1-908177-92-6

Social history
Victorian Servants *Fiona Macdonald* 978-1-907184-49-9

North of the Border
Scottish Clans *Fiona Macdonald* 978-1-908759-90-0
Scottish Tartan and Highland Dress
    Fiona Macdonald 978-1-908759-89-4
Scottish Words *Fiona Macdonald* 978-1-908759-63-4
Whisky *Fiona Macdonald* 978-1-907184-76-5

British places
Brighton *David Arscott* 978-1-906714-89-5
London *Jim Pipe* 978-1-907184-26-0
Yorkshire *John Malam* 978-1-907184-57-4

Famous Britons
Great Britons *Ian Graham* 978-1-907184-59-8
Robert Burns *Fiona Macdonald* 978-1-908177-71-1
Charles Dickens *Fiona Macdonald* 978-1-908177-15-5
William Shakespeare *Jacqueline Morley* 978-1-908177-15-5

Sports and pastimes
Cricket *Jim Pipe* 978-1-908177-90-2
Fishing *Rob Beattie* 978-1-908177-91-9
Golf *David Arscott* 978-1-907184-75-8
The Olympics *David Arscott* 978-1-907184-78-9
The World Cup *David Arscott* 978-1-907184-38-3

Royalty
Kings & Queens of Great Britain
   Antony Mason 978-1-906714-77-2
Royal Weddings *Fiona Macdonald* 978-1-907184-84-0
The Tudors *Jim Pipe* 978-1-907184-58-1
Queen Elizabeth II Diamond Jubilee:
   60 Years a Queen *David Arscott* 978-1-908177-50-6

Natural history
Cats *Fiona Macdonald* 978-1-908973-34-4
Dogs *Fiona Macdonald* 978-1-908973-35-1
Global Warming *Ian Graham* 978-1-907184-51-2

Ancient and medieval history
Ancient Egypt: Mummy Myth and Magic
   Jim Pipe 978-1-906714-92-5
Castles *Jacqueline Morley* 978-1-907184-48-2

Folklore and traditions
Christmas *Fiona Macdonald* 978-1-907184-50-5
Vampires *Fiona Macdonald* 978-1-907184-39-0

Myths and legends

Heroes, Gods and Monsters of Celtic Mythology
   Fiona Macdonald 978-1-905638-97-0